BEING JOHN MALKOVICH
Charlie Kaufman

ff

faber and faber

Faber and Faber, Inc.
An affiliate of Farrar, Straus and Giroux
18 West 18th Street, New York 10011

Copyright © 1999 by Universal Studios Publishing Rights,
a division of Universal Studios Licensing Inc.
Being John Malkovich is a trademark and copyright of Universal Studios
All rights reserved
Printed in the United States of America
Originally published in 2000 by Faber and Faber Limited,
3 Queen Square, London WCIN 3AU
Published in the United States by Faber and Faber, Inc.
First American edition, 2000

A CIP record for this book is available from the British Library
Library of Congress Control Number: 2003427888

ISBN-13: 978-0-571-20586-8
ISBN-10: 0-571-20586-0

www.fsgbooks.com

8   10   12   14   15   13   11   9

BEING JOHN MALKOVICH

CONTENTS

INTRODUCTION
by Charlie Kaufman

They asked me to write an introduction to this screenplay. I told them I didn't know what to say. They told me it didn't matter, just something. They said people studying screenwriting often purchase these books and they'll be looking for a word from the writer. They told me I owed the readers something. I said I would try. I prefer not to owe people. So I am sitting here tonight trying. It's three in the morning. I haven't been able to sleep for several weeks now. Things are falling apart. I have personal problems. Perhaps I've been drinking too much. This was suggested to me by someone I once considered a friend. The point is, things are confused. For a while I was living out of my car. I was in transition. The place I had been living was no longer an option. People are funny. Don't trust them. So I was in my car, which was parked in the driveway of an acquaintance, an out-of-work actor, who was helping me out. I could've stayed in a hotel. That is, I could've afforded to stay in a hotel, but I didn't. I needed someplace familiar or I would've lost what was left of my mind. My car is familiar. It's had the same fast food wrappers on the floor for the past five months. They're sort of like friends. How's it goin' today, McDonald's? What's up, Starbucks cups? In the mornings I showered in the actor's bathroom. It wasn't a bad deal. He has a pretty girlfriend and sometimes she'd smile at me. Nothing provocative. Nothing like that, but it got me through some of the tougher days. Now I'm in a place. I rented a small apartment. It's fine until I work out some of the issues I need to work out. But living here and being somewhat isolated has taken a toll. I'm not thinking clearly. My work has suffered. I have bad thoughts. The man across the hall is old and sad. He sometimes asks me in for tea. I always decline and then feel guilty and miserable about it, but not enough to go and have a goddamn cup of tea with him. This is beside the point. The point is an introduction. What can I say about *Being John Malkovich*? I wrote it several years ago for no reason at all. I don't know why I chose

John Malkovich. I don't know how I came up with the idea. I don't have answers to any of that. I don't have any answers. I'm a man without answers. He said somewhat histrionically. Sometimes, when it's late enough and dark enough and quiet enough, I am even a man without questions. A lack of curiosity, a numbness creeps over me and I just sit. I stare at that weird, suspicious stain on the wall and think of nothing. I don't wonder about the universe. Then a little question will slowly bore its way to the front of my brain. The question is why am I in this situation? Who am I that is so terrible that people must respond to me with such brutality? Yes, brutality. A brutality of spirit. I am a person. I have my weaknesses, certainly. My insecurities, my desires. But I have a right to them. I'm not going to let anyone tell me otherwise. So if the price I have to pay for living my life is to be cast out, then I guess that is the price I have to pay. But I don't have to be Little Mary Sunshine about it. Perhaps this is not what I am to share with you, a stranger who has just innocently purchased this screenplay. Perhaps this is not what you want to read. Perhaps you want to know about Hollywood or the writing process or some such nonsense. Perhaps you'd like to read a cute anecdote about one of the actors in the film or you'd like to know who slept with whom or you'd like me to be clever or you'd like me to tell you the character of Lester was based on my high-school algebra teacher. But I don't have it in me to give you any of that. I have nothing cute or sparkling or insightful to say. I am a miserably lonely person who has no charming anecdotes. The only thing I can talk about, the only thing that's on my mind at the moment is that the human being can be a treacherous creature. And that sometimes they can tell you they love you and they care about you and maybe they don't. How terrible is that, to come to that realization? Of course it makes sense. Nobody could really like me. I mean, nobody ever has before. So I sell a screenplay and suddenly someone likes me. Just a coincidence, right? Yeah, right. If there's anything I can say about screenwriting in this introduction, it's that you need to write what you know. And I don't know anything. I don't understand a damn second of my life. I exist in a fog of confusion and anxiety and clutching jealousy and loneliness. The old man across the hall, in his own hell, is reaching out to me to offer comfort and perhaps with some insane hope that I might comfort him. But I won't accept his invitation. He's not a beautiful babe who wants to fuck me because she saw my name in an article in one of the trade papers. I have no use for him. I make myself sick. God, the sun is coming up already. There's traffic on the street. Actual human beings going to actual jobs. What must that be like? I hear the old man knocking around his room, his whistling teakettle mocking me. And I'm no closer to figuring out this introduction. Or anything else. What can I tell you about the screenwriting process as I know it? Just maybe that you're alone in this. Take your inspiration where you find it. I don't even know what that means. Inspiration? What the hell is inspiration, anyway? You just sit there and wait. That's all I do. I sit and wait. I don't even know for what. For it to get better? What is *it*? You tell me? You write an introduction and send it to me. Maybe you know. Maybe you can tell me something. Why does it always have to go in this direction, writer to reader? Maybe you have the one thought that'll change everything for me. The one thing I haven't considered in my relentless, obsessive, circular thought process. Is there that one thing? Is it possible for one person to impart any transformative notion to another person? Is that what I'm supposed to offer to you in this introduction? Something to start you off on the road to a successful screenwriting career? Awfully presumptuous of me to think I might have that capability. Awfully naïve of you to expect it. Look, the truth is everything is a mess as far as I can tell. It's just a messy, junky world. People are mean. People are lonely. People are lost. Nobody knows a damn thing. Some people pretend they do. Don't trust them. Some people pretend they like you. Don't believe them. And if you're going to write a screenplay, try to keep it around a hundred and ten pages.

Charlie Kaufman
Los Angeles, California

Crap. That's my big finish? It's nothing. Almost like a joke. It's a punchline and not a very good one. I should be ashamed. Here you are, probably a decent person. Maybe you liked this movie and wanted to read the script, get a sense of the writing and the writer, and here I am in my furnished room with my utter and complete self-indulgence, making light of your sincere curiosity as I spew my contaminated, bilious psyche onto you. Like a virus-filled sneeze. I apologize to you. I apologize to everyone I've ever had anything to do with. I owe you at least one clean, true thought on the craft of screenwriting. I see that now. Otherwise I could never forgive myself. Otherwise I am a completely odious person. And I can't be that. I just can't. So, look, y'know, it's hard to say anything concrete. I guess the one important thing to me in my work is to tell the truth. I guess. I guess that's it. But why do I want to tell the truth? Maybe so I can be known as the guy who tells the truth. Maybe it's nothing more than that. Just more self-aggrandizement masquerading as honesty. It's my shtick. Hey, I'll be the guy who tells it like it is. Maybe then someone will love me. Maybe some woman will find that sexy. I mean, I'm not going to get them with my looks. So I'm the honest one. Hey, look at me! I tell the goddamn truth no matter what the consequences! What a fucking hero. I'm sorry. I guess that didn't go where I had hoped. Listen, I'm just an insignificant guy who wants to be significant. I want to be loved and admired. I want women to think I'm sexy. Even men. That'd be fine, too. I want everyone to think I'm brilliant. *And* I want them all to think I don't care about any of that stuff. There you go. Who I am. Now I'd better get down to the Kinko's in Glendale and e-mail this to Faber and Faber before I change my chickenshit mind.

Charlie Kaufman
Los Angeles, California

Finally, I want to thank all the people who worked so hard to turn this screenplay into a movie. It was an arduous process and the creativity and tireless work of everyone involved was an absolute joy to witness.

Charlie Kaufman
Glendale, California

CAST AND CREW

MAIN CAST

CRAIG SCHWARTZ	John Cusack
LOTTE SCHWARTZ	Cameron Diaz
MAXINE	Catherine Keener
DR LESTER	Orson Bean
FLORIS	Mary Kay Place
ERROLL	W. Earl Brown
LARRY THE AGENT	Carlos Jacott
GUY IN RESTAURANT	Willie Garson
CAPTAIN MERTIN	Byrne Piven
MAN IN BAR	Gregory Sporleder
CHARLIE	Charlie Sheen
JOHN HORATIO MALKOVICH	John Malkovich

MAIN CREW

Directed by	Spike Jonze
Written by	Charlie Kaufman
Produced by	Michael Stipe
	and Sandy Stern
Produced by	Steve Golin
	Vincent Landay
Executive Producers	Charlie Kaufman
	Michael Kuhn
Original Music	Carter Burwell
Cinematography	Lance Acord
Film Editing	Eric Zumbrunnen
Production Design	K. K. Barrett
Costume Design	Casey Storm

EXT. NEW YORK CITY STREETS (MONTAGE) – DAY

The montage plays under the opening credits. It feels real, shot documentary style.

We watch Craig, 30 years old, in various locations, at various times of day, and in several different changes of clothes, attempting to earn money as a street puppeteer. His act consists of following passers-by and imitating their mannerisms and gaits with his marionette (a delicately crafted miniature version of himself). Craig is amazingly skilled, his puppet's impersonations are letter perfect. But the people he's imitating either ignore his efforts, hurry to get past, or yell at him to leave them alone. His change cup remains empty.

EXT. NYC SUBWAY ENTRANCE – NIGHT

The last shot in the sequence is of Craig at night, heading down into a subway entrance, his marionette slung dejectedly over his shoulder.

FADE TO BLACK:

VOICE
Craig, honey, time to wake up.

CUT TO:

INT. CRAIG AND LOTTE'S BEDROOM – MORNING

Craig jolts awake in bed. An African grey parrot stands on his chest staring at him.

PARROT
Craig, honey, time to wake up.

Lotte, 30, in the middle of dressing for work, hurries in and pulls the bird from Craig's chest.

LOTTE

Sorry, hon. I didn't know Orrin Hatch was out of his cage. Good morning.

Lotte leans down and kisses Craig on the forehead.

CRAIG

Morning.

LOTTE

Gotta run, sorry. Shipment of meal worms coming in first thing.

CRAIG

Enjoy.

LOTTE

Craig, listen, honey, I've been thinking . . . Maybe you'd feel better if you got, you know, a job or something.

CRAIG

We've been over this. Nobody's looking for a puppeteer in today's wintry economic climate.

LOTTE

Well, you know, maybe something else until this whole puppet thing turns around.

CRAIG
(*bitterly*)
The Great Mantini doesn't need a day job.

LOTTE
(*sighs*)
Craig, everyone can't be Derek Mantini.
(*beat*)
Well, meal worms are waiting. Do me a favor?

CRAIG

What?

LOTTE

Would you check in on Elijah? He seems to be a little under the weather this morning.

                              CRAIG
Which one is Elijah again?

                              LOTTE
The monkey.

                              CRAIG
Yeah. Okay.

                                                          CUT TO:

INT. CRAIG AND LOTTE'S STORAGE ROOM – MORNING

The place is a mess. Bartók blasts through cheap speakers. A small marionette stage stands in the back of the storage room. The stage is lit and on it is the 'Craig' puppet pacing back and forth, wringing its hands with incredible subtlety. We see Craig, above and behind the stage. He is manipulating the puppet. His fingers move fast and furious. The puppet breaks into a dance, a beautiful and intricate balletic piece. Soon the puppet is leaping and tumbling through space, moves that one would think impossible for a marionette. Sweat appears on the real Craig's brow. His fingers move like lightning. The Craig puppet wipes its brow. The puppet moves faster and faster, finally collapsing on the floor of the stage. It puts its hands up to its face and weeps. Craig hangs the puppet, and comes down around the front of the stage. He is heaving. He switches off the music, picks up a beer and takes a swig.

                                                          CUT TO:

INT. CRAIG AND LOTTE'S LIVING-ROOM – DAY

The room is filled with penned and unpenned animals of all kinds: a snake, an iguana, the parrot, a dog, cats, etc. Craig, sits on the couch flipping through the paper. He turns to the want ads. The TV is on in the background. Elijah, the monkey, sits next to Craig, holding his stomach and moaning weakly.

On the TV, Derek Mantini is working a 60-foot high marionette from the top of a water tower. The assembled crowd is enthralled.

                        TV ANNOUNCER
The crowd is enthralled as Derek Mantini, arguably the
greatest puppeteer in the history of the world, performs *The*

Belle of Amherst with his 60-foot Emily Dickinson puppet, directed by the inimitable Charles Nelson Reilly.

Charles Nelson Reilly floats by the tower in a hot-air balloon.

CHARLES NELSON REILLY
Beautiful, beautiful! Nyong-nyong.

CRAIG
Gimmicky bastard.

Elijah moans. Craig looks at him.

You don't know how lucky you are being a monkey. If I were a monkey, I'd be the happiest man alive. Nobody expecting anything of me. Just sit on a couch and moan all day. That's the life.

Elijah glances up at Craig, quizzically. Craig tries to stare him down, gives up.

CUT TO:

EXT. WASHINGTON SQUARE PARK – DAY

Craig has set up a portable puppet stage and is in the middle of a performance. A few people watch. A placard on an easel next to the stage reads: 'The tragedy of Abelard and Heloise.' There is a hat with coins in it. The puppet stage set is two medieval rooms divided by a wall. Each room features a writing desk. Craig works two puppets. One is dressed as a medieval nun (Heloise), the other as a monk (Abelard). Each sits writing at a desk. A boom box plays the voices of Abelard and Heloise.

HELOISE
While we enjoyed the pleasures of an uneasy love and abandoned ourselves to fornication, we were spared God's severity . . .

A man walks by with his young daughter.

LITTLE GIRL
Daddy, a puppet show.

4

ABELARD

Say no more, I beg you, and cease from complaints like
these . . .

FATHER
(*looking at his watch*)
Just for a minute, honey, we gotta meet mommy.

*The two stop. The girl runs excitedly right up to the little stage. The
father sits on a bench.*

HELOISE

Even during the celebration of the Mass, when our prayers
should be purer . . .

*Heloise rises from her desk and walks to the wall separating her from
Abelard. Abelard moves to his side of the wall.*

. . . lewd visions of these pleasures take such a hold upon my
unhappy soul that my thoughts are on their wantonness
instead of my prayers.

*The puppets begin making love to each other as if the wall were not
there. The father, who has not been paying attention, looks up. He
watches as the two puppets gyrate more and more sexually.*

Sometimes my thoughts are betrayed in a movement of my
body . . .

The father's eyes widen.

FATHER

Holy fuck!

*He storms the stage, knocking over the cardboard set, crushing a puppet.
He slugs Craig in the face.*

CUT TO:

INT. PET STORE – EVENING

*Lotte, in a smock, is in the back, feeding fish. The doorbell jingles as
someone enters the shop. Lotte looks up. It's Craig. His lip is swollen
and his nose is bloody. He drags his puppet behind him. The puppet's
head is partially crushed. Lotte gasps and runs over to Craig.*

5

LOTTE

Oh, sweetheart, not again! Oh, sweetie. Are you okay?

Craig shrugs. Lotte hugs him.

Craiggy, why are you doing this to yourself?

CRAIG
(*through fat lip*)

I uh puppeteeh.

Lotte looks at him, her eyes brimming with tears.

CUT TO:

INT. CRAIG AND LOTTE'S STORAGE ROOM – MORNING

Craig sits at his workbench, holding the now detached crushed puppet head. He stares at it, his repair tools at the ready. He sighs, and puts the head in a drawer.

CUT TO:

INT. KITCHEN – MORNING

Close-up of a newspaper opening. We pull back to see Craig at the kitchen table looking at the job classifieds. He checks under 'Puppeteers'. Nothing. A boxed ad with the bold-type heading 'Looking for a man with fast hands' catches Craig's eye. He reads the ad: 'short-statured file clerk with unusually nimble and dexterous fingers needed for speed filing. EOE.' Craig writes down the address.

EXT. MERTIN-FLEMMER BUILDING – DAY

Craig, in a sports coat and tie, walks down 11th Avenue, checking addresses.

CUT TO:

INT. OFFICE BUILDING LOBBY – DAY

Craig, studies the business listings board. He finds LesterCorp, and sees that it is located on floor $7\frac{1}{2}$. Craig presses the elevator button and waits. A woman comes and waits next to him. The doors open, and Craig and the woman get in.

CUT TO:

INT. ELEVATOR – CONTINUOUS

The woman presses '9'. Craig studies the buttons. There is no '7½'.

WOMAN #1

Seven and a half, right?

CRAIG

Uh, yeah.

WOMAN #1

I'll take you through it.

The woman picks up a crowbar leaning in the corner. She watches the floor numbers light up in succession. After '7' and before '8', the woman hits the emergency stop button. The elevator slams to a halt. The woman pries open the doors with the crowbar. Revealed is a standard office building hallway, except that from floor to ceiling it is only about four feet high. Everything is scaled down accordingly. The number on the wall across from the elevator is 7½.

WOMAN #1

Seven and a half.

CRAIG

Thank you.

Craig climbs out on to the 7½ floor.

CUT TO:

INT. 7½ FLOOR – CONTINUOUS

Craig, hunched-over, makes his way down the hallway, looking for LesterCorp. He passes a hunched-over man walking in the other direction. They nod to each other. Craig finds a door marked 'LesterCorp – Meeting America's Filing Needs Since 1922'. He enters.

CUT TO:

INT. LESTERCORP RECEPTION AREA – CONTINUOUS

All furniture is scaled down to fit into this low-ceilinged space. A few other men sit reading magazines. Employees hustle by carrying boxes of filed materials. Craig approaches Floris, the receptionist.

> **FLORIS**
> Welcome to LesterCorp. May we meet your filing needs?

> **CRAIG**
> No, uh, my name is Craig Schwartz. I have an interview with Mr Lester.

> **FLORIS**
> Please have a seat, Mr Juarez . . .

> **CRAIG**
> Schwartz.

> **FLORIS**
> Pardon?

> **CRAIG**
> Schwartz.

> **FLORIS**
> I'm sorry, I'm afraid I have no idea what you're saying right now.

> **CRAIG**
> My name is Schwartz.

> **FLORIS**
> Money, Miss Warts?

> **CRAIG**
> Forget it.

Craig takes a seat next to the other applicants.

> **FLORIS**
> (*calling across the room*)
> For credit?

The intercom buzzes. Floris picks it up.

> **FLORIS**
> (*to Craig*)
> Mr Juarez?

8

CRAIG

Yes?

FLORIS

Chest?

CRAIG

I said 'yes'.

FLORIS

You suggest *what*? I have no time for piddling suggestions from mumbling job applicants, my good man. Besides, Dr Lester will see you now.

INT. LESTER'S OFFICE – CONTINUOUS

Craig enters. Lester, a giant of an old man, sits hunched in his tiny chair.

LESTER

Come in, Mr Juarez. I'd stand, but, well, you know.

CRAIG
(*extending his hand*)
Actually, my name is Craig Schwartz, Dr Lester.

Lester flips an intercom switch.

LESTER

Security.

CRAIG

No, it's okay, sir. Just a mix-up with your secretary.

LESTER

She's not my secretary. She's what they call an executive liaison, and I'm not banging her, if that's what you're implying.

CRAIG

Not at all, Dr Lester. I simply misspoke.

LESTER

Tell me, Dr Schwartz, what do you feel you can bring to LesterCorp?

CRAIG

Well, sir, I'm an excellent filer.

LESTER
(*crafty*)

You think so, eh?

Lester pulls out two index cards, concentrates, then scribbles something on each card.

Okay, which letter comes first . . .

Lester holds up both cards. On the right card is a letter 'M', on the left card is a strange, indecipherable symbol.

. . . this or this?

CRAIG

The symbol on the left is not a letter, sir.

LESTER

Damn, you *are* good. I tried to trick you. Okay, put these in order.

Lester hands Craig a bunch of index cards. Craig orders them with amazing speed and dexterity. Lester watches, eyes wide.

(*flips intercom switch*)
Floris, get Guinness on the phone.

FLORIS
(*off-screen*)

Genghis Khan Capone?

LESTER

Forget it.

FLORIS
(*off-screen*)

For credit?

LESTER
(*flips off switch*)
Fine woman, Floris. I don't know how she puts up with this damn speech impediment of mine.

CRAIG

You don't have a speech impediment, Dr Lester.

LESTER

Flattery will get you everywhere, my boy. But I'm afraid I
have to trust Floris on this one. You see, she has her
doctorate in speech impedimentology from Case Western.
Perhaps you've read her memoirs, *I Can't Understand A Word
Any Of You Are Saying.*

CRAIG

No.

LESTER

Pity, it tells it like it is. That's why the eastern, read Jewish,
publishing establishment won't touch it. That's a quote from
the book jacket. George Will, I think.
(*beat*)
I apologize if you can't understand a word I'm saying, Dr
Schwartz.

CRAIG

No. I understand perfectly.

LESTER
(*choking up*)
Thank you for being kind enough to lie. You see, I've been
very lonely in my isolated tower of indecipherable speech.
You're hired. Any questions?

CRAIG

Just one. Why is this floor so short?

LESTER

Low overhead, m'boy. We pass the savings on to you.
(*laughs heartily*)
But seriously, that's all covered in orientation.

CUT TO:

INT. 7½ FLOOR – DAY

Craig walks down the hall. He enters the orientation room.

INT. ORIENTATION ROOM – DAY

It's a conference room. There are a few people scattered about. Craig sits. He looks around and his eyes rest on Maxine. She is in her late twenties with close-cropped black hair. Her eyes are opaque, her face expressionless, her countenance trance-like. She appears to be using the orientation room as a break room. She smokes a cigarette and reads a magazine. Craig is fixated. Maxine glances over at him, then turns back to her magazine. The lights dim. A video monitor is illuminated.

CUT TO:

EXT. OFFICE BUILDING – DAY

We tilt up the building.

MUSIC: *perky industrial film music*

Title: THE $7\frac{1}{2}$ FLOOR

NARRATOR
(*voice-over*)

Welcome to the $7\frac{1}{2}$ floor of the Mertin-Flemmer building. As you will now be spending your work day here, it is important that you learn a bit about the history of this famous floor.

DISSOLVE TO:

INT. $7\frac{1}{2}$ FLOOR – DAY

Don and Wendy, two office workers, crouch in the hall and chat. Both hold cups of coffee.

WENDY

Hello, Don.

DON

Hello, Wendy.

WENDY

Don, I was wondering, do you know why our workplace has such low ceilings?

DON

It's an interesting story, Wendy. Many years ago in the late

1800s, James Mertin, an Irish ship captain looking to invest in the future of our great country, came to this town and decided to erect an office building.

                                                    CUT TO:

OLD FOOTAGE OF CONSTRUCTION CREW WORKING

                          DON
                       (*voice-over*)
He would call this building the Mertin-Flemmer Building, after himself and someone else, who, local legend has it, was named Flemmer.

                                                    CUT TO:

INT. NINETEENTH-CENTURY OFFICE – DAY

An actor playing Mertin sits at a desk and writes with a quill. He appears very stern and has mutton chop sideburns.

                          DON
                       (*voice-over*)
One day, Captain Mertin received an unexpected visitor.

There is a knock at the door.

                        MERTIN
Enter ye, if ye dare enter.

A tiny woman enters.

                      TINY WOMAN
Captain Mertin?

                        MERTIN
What want ye, girl child?

                      TINY WOMAN
I am not a child, Captain Mertin, but rather an adult lady of miniature proportions.

MERTIN
(*taken aback*)

I see. Well, it is not my fault that thou art tiny. So if it is
charity yer after, then be gone with ye, ye foul demon.

TINY WOMAN

I am not asking for alms, but rather the ear of a kind man
with a noble heart.

MERTIN
(*sighs*)

Aye. Speak then if ye must.

TINY WOMAN

Captain Mertin, surely I am a God-fearing Christian woman
like yourself, but, alas, I am afraid that the world was not built
with me in mind. Doorknobs are too high, chairs are
unwieldy, high-ceilinged rooms mock my stature. Nor am I a
married lady, Captain. After all, who would marry a person of
my diminutiveness? So I am forced to work for my few
pennies a week as an optometrist. Why cannot there be a
place for me to work safe and comfortable?

Mertin wipes a tear from his eye.

MERTIN

Woman, your story moves me like no other. Me own sister
was tiny and then died. Therefore, I shall make ye me wife.
And I shall build a floor in my building, between the seventh
and eighth, which will be scaled down, so from now on there
shall be at least one place on God's green Earth that you and
your accursed kind can live in peace . . .

DISSOLVE TO:

INT. HALLWAY 7½ FLOOR – DAY

Don and Wendy crouch and talk.

DON

So that's the story of 7½ . Since the rents are considerably
lower, this floor has been adopted by businesses which for

one reason of another are forced to cut corners. After all . . .
the overhead is low! Ha ha ha!

> WENDY

Ha ha ha!

TITLE: *The End*

CUT TO:

INT. ORIENTATION ROOM – DAY

The monitor goes dark. The lights go up. Craig looks over at Maxine.
She stands and walks past him.

> CRAIG

Moving story.

> MAXINE

Unfortunately the story is bullshit.

> CRAIG

Is that true?

> MAXINE

Truth is for suckers, isn't it?

> CRAIG

Listen, I'm Craig Schwartz, just starting out at LesterCorp.
Where are you just starting out?

> MAXINE

How dreary – to be – Somebody / How public – like a Frog /
To tell one's name – the livelong June / To an admiring Bog!

> CRAIG
> (*proudly*)

Emily Dickinson.

> MAXINE

I wouldn't know.

Maxine walks away.

CUT TO:

INT. CRAIG AND LOTTE'S KITCHEN – NIGHT

Lotte chops onions. A parrot sits on her head. Craig stirs a pot on the stove. A monkey leaps from the top of the cabinet to the top of the refrigerator to the kitchen table. A dog watches the monkey and barks at it.

> PARROT
>
> Shut up! Shut up! Shut up!

> CRAIG
>
> Shut up!

> LOTTE
> (*to Craig*)
>
> Sorry, honey.

The dog continues to bark.

> PARROT
>
> Sorry honey. Sorry honey.

An offscreen neighbor pounds the wall.

> NEIGHBOR
> (*off-screen*)
>
> Shut up!

> LOTTE
> (*yelling*)
>
> Sorry!

Lotte grabs the parrot off her head and leaves the room.

> PARROT
> (*off-screen*)
> Help! She's locking me in a cage!

Lotte re-enters.

> LOTTE
> Isn't that cute? I just taught him that.

> CRAIG
> Adorable. What time are they supposed to be here?

                                   LOTTE
Sevenish.

                                   CRAIG
We have to make it an early night.

                                   LOTTE
They'll understand. Besides I've got a morning appointment
tomorrow with Elijah's shrink. We're getting to the bottom of
this acid stomach.

                                   CRAIG
                              (*not paying attention*)
Hmmm.

                                   LOTTE
Some sort of childhood trauma, she thinks. Possible feelings
of inadequacy as a chimp. Interesting, huh?

                                   CRAIG
Hmmm.

                                   LOTTE
                                  (*beat*)
So, honey, have you thought any more about having a baby?

                                   CRAIG
You know, it's so tough right now. Economically and all.
We'll see if the job things pays off.

*Lotte nods halfheartedly. The doorbell rings. The dog barks. The parrot
screams. The neighbor pounds on the wall.*

                                                        DISSOLVE TO:

INT. CRAIG AND LOTTE'S DINING-ROOM – NIGHT

*The dining-room table is set up. Craig and Lotte and their friends Peter
and Gloria are seated and eating dinner. There is an obvious lull in the
conversation.*

                                   PETER
Good food, Lotte.

LOTTE

Thanks. Craig helped, too, by the way.

PETER

Vegetarian, right?

LOTTE

Yes. All vegetable, all the time.

PETER

Amazing.

There is another lull. Everyone eats.

No kidding about that $7\frac{1}{2}$ floor, Craig?

CRAIG

No kidding, Peter.

GLORIA

That's great. It almost sounds like make-believe.
                    (*beat*)
Like a story-book.
                    (*beat*)
Like a fairy-tale.
                    (*beat*)
It's really great.
                    (*beat*)
So, Lotte, when you say all vegetable, do you mean all
vegetable *entirely*?

CUT TO:

INT. TAXI CAB – NIGHT

Gloria and Peter are riding in silence.

GLORIA

Lotte told me that Eskimos have a lot of words for snow.

PETER

How many?

GLORIA

Twenty-three. No, twenty-seven, I think.

PETER

I wonder why so many.

GLORIA

Because they have a lot of snow. Isn't that interesting?

CUT TO:

INT. CRAIG AND LOTTE'S KITCHEN – NIGHT

Craig washes the dishes. Lotte dries them. They don't look at each other.

CUT TO:

INT. LESTERCORP WORK AREA – MORNING

Craig, in a cream-colored suit, is pushing a cart with files, dropping them off on people's desks. Floris watches from the doorway.

FLORIS

You're good.

Craig turns.

CRAIG
(*over-enunciating*)

Thank you, Floris.

Floris shrugs, shakes her head.

FLORIS

You're not like the other boys we've had here. Granted, I can't understand what you're saying either, but your soft palette resonates tremendously well and you never ever constrict your epiglottis.

CRAIG

I *am* a trained performer.

FLORIS
(*swooning*)

Music to my ears! Whatever you said. Speak, speak, speak, my magnificent friend, speak!

INT. BREAKFAST-ROOM/HALLWAY 7½ FLOOR – DAY

Craig pours himself a cup of coffee. Maxine approaches with an empty cup.

> CRAIG

Hello again.

Craig fills her cup.

> MAXINE

Yes, well . . .

> CRAIG

You know, I've been thinking about what you said yesterday, about the orientation film story being bullshit. I think you're on to something.

> MAXINE

And fifty *other* lines to get into a girl's pants.

> CRAIG

No, really.

> MAXINE

You know, if you ever got me, you wouldn't have a clue what to do with me. That's the thing, Romeo.

Maxine walks away.

CUT TO:

INT. CRAIG AND LOTTE'S STORAGE ROOM – NIGHT

Craig is at his workbench, painting the finishing touches on a new puppet. It is beautiful. It is Maxine. We see that he has already repaired the Craig puppet head. It sits, still wet with paint, on a sheet of newspaper. Lotte observes all of this quietly from the door. A Lotte puppet hangs from a hook, tangled and dusty.

> LOTTE

New puppet?

Craig is surprised, caught.

CRAIG

Yeah, just an idea I had.

LOTTE

She's very beautiful.

CRAIG
(*shrugging*)

Just an idea I had.

Craig hangs the puppet, stands, and switches off the light.

C'mon, let's go to bed.

CUT TO:

INT. CRAIG AND LOTTE'S BEDROOM – NIGHT

The room is dark. Lotte snores lightly. Craig lies there with his eyes open. Quietly, he gets up and leaves the bedroom. Lotte watches him go.

CUT TO:

INT. CRAIG AND LOTTE'S STORAGE ROOM – NIGHT

Craig stands above the puppet stage. He is working both the Craig puppet and the Maxine puppet at the same time. The two perform a beautiful and graceful pas de deux. They finish in a passionate embrace.

CRAIG
(*quietly*)

I would *too* know what to do with you.

CUT TO:

INT. LESTERCORP WORK AREA – MORNING

Craig files. Floris watches him from the doorway. Dr Lester watches Floris from behind a cabinet.

FLORIS

Oh, what magic those fingers could work on the right 'cabinet'.

(*strokes Craig's neck*)
Alphabetize *me*, baby. And don't forget, *I* comes before *U*.

Floris laughs long and hard. Too long and too hard.

CRAIG

Floris, you're very nice, but I'm afraid I'm in love with somebody else.

FLORIS
(*upset*)

I'm afraid I . . . have no idea what you are saying . . . you bastard!

Floris runs from the room. Lester pokes his head out from behind the cabinet.

LESTER

Don't toy with Floris, Schwartz. Why, if I were eighty years younger, I'd box your ears.

CRAIG

I wasn't toying with her, sir. I was just . . . How old *are* you?

LESTER

One hundred and five. Carrot juice.
(*beat*)

Lots of it. I swear, it's almost not worth it. I piss orange. Oh, and I have to piss sitting down . . . like a goddamn girly girl . . . every fifteen minutes. But nobody wants to die, Schwartz.

CRAIG

I'll keep that in mind, sir.

LESTER

No sir-ee-bob, I don't die. But what I do is get older, wrinkled like a former plum that's become the wrinkled prune you see before you. Oh, to be a young man again, maybe then Floris would care for me.

CRAIG

The elderly have so much to offer, sir. They are our link with history.

LESTER

I don't want to be your goddamn link, damn you. I want to
feel Floris' naked thighs against my own. I want to know
passion. I want my body to inspire lust in that beautiful,
complex woman. I want her to shiver in a spasm of ecstasy
when I penetrate her. Oh, God, the agony of the flesh,
Schwartz.

CRAIG

Dr Lester, while I am flattered that you share your feelings
with me, I believe perhaps the workplace is not the most
suitable environment for this type of discussion.

LESTER

All right. Meet me at the Juicy-Juice Juice Bar after work
today and I'll spill my goddamn guts for you.

Lester exits.

CRAIG

Shit.

CUT TO:

INT. HALLWAY 7½ FLOOR – DAY

*Craig squats next to a payphone. As he talks, he watches a small group
of really old people step out of the elevator and head into the LesterCorp
office.*

CRAIG
(*into phone*)

I won't be late, Lot. I just have to listen to Lester's sexual
fantasies and drink carrot juice for a little while. It's a job
thing.

*Maxine walks by. Craig grabs her arm, signals for her to wait a
minute. She waits.*

(*into phone*)

I gotta go back to work. Yeah, okay. You too. Okay. Bye.

Craig hangs up.

MAXINE

What?

CRAIG

I just wanted to say 'hi'. Did you know I still don't know your name or where you work?

MAXINE

Yeah.

CRAIG

How about this, if I can guess your first name within three tries, you have to come out for a drink with me tonight.

MAXINE

Why not?

CRAIG

Great.

(watches her face as he guesses)

Buuuhhppaahhhhnnn . . . Muhhhahhhhh . . . Mahhhnnnaaa . . . nollltuuukkkaaaaralllll . . . tashabarbarasssssssuuuuus aaaaaaannnnnnnaaaaaannnnnnnnnnnnncccccceeeeeee . . . Mwaaaaaa . . . Mahhhhhkkkkk . . . sssseeeeeen. Maxine?

MAXINE

Who told you?

CRAIG

I'm right?

MAXINE

Who told you?

CRAIG

I was right? Nobody told me, Maxine! God, doesn't it seem like this must mean something or something? Like some kind of, y'know, psychic connection between us? I don't know, I don't know. It means something! Maxine! Jesus, what a beautiful name! Maxine. Maxine. I could say it all day!

MAXINE

Somebody told you.

CRAIG

No, nobody told me, Maxine. It just came out of me. This is so amazing. So where do you live and stuff?

MAXINE

I am dubious, but I don't welsh. Meet me at The Stuck Pig. Seven o'clock. You're late, I walk. So help me, if I find out you cheated.

CRAIG
(*in heaven*)

Maxine.

Craig walks down the hall. A tiny smile flits across Maxine's face.

CUT TO:

INT. JUICY-JUICE JUICE BAR – EVENING

Lester and Craig sit at a table. There are several emptied glasses of carrot juice in front of Lester. Craig nurses one glass, and keeps checking his watch.

LESTER

Imagine a room full of women. Nubile, blonde, wet with desire, Schwartz. A harem, if you will. Me in leather. A harness, if you like. I am the object of this desire, and all eyes are on me as I speak. 'Ladies,' I begin, 'I am the love god, Eros. I intoxicate you. My spunk is to you manna from heaven . . .'

CRAIG
(*standing*)

Dr Lester, it's been really fascinating, but I'm afraid I have to get home to my wife now.

LESTER

Wife, huh? I'd love to meet her, Craig.

CRAIG

Yessir.

LESTER

Shall we say dinner on Thursday.

> (afterthought)
> You can come too if you like.
> (beat)
> That was a joke, Schwartz. Get it? You can come, too. See
> what I did there?

                    CRAIG
                 (checking watch)
> That's good, sir. Gotta run.

*Craig hurries to the door. Lester downs Craig's juice, signals the waiter
for more.*

                                        CUT TO:

INT. THE STUCK PIG – NIGHT

*The interior design is Japanese and austere. Maxine sits at the bar,
watching her watch. Aside from Maxine, everyone else in the room is
Japanese. Craig rushes in, frantic, out of breath. He spots Maxine and
plops himself next to her.*

                    CRAIG
> Made it, Maxine. Maxine, Maxine, Maxine.

                    MAXINE
> Just.

                    CRAIG
> Buy you a drink, Maxine?

                    MAXINE
> You married?

                    CRAIG
> Yeah. But enough about me.

Maxine laughs. The bartender approaches.

                    CRAIG
> What'll you have?

                    MAXINE
                 (to bartender)
> The usual, Barry.

CRAIG
(*to bartender*)
I'll have, like, a beer. Like a Budweiser, or something.

The bartender walks away.

I like you. I don't know what it is exactly.

MAXINE
My tits?

CRAIG
No, no, it's your energy or your attitude or the way you carry
yourself or . . .

MAXINE
Christ, you're not a fag, are you? Because I don't want to be
wasting my time.

CRAIG
No, I'm . . .

*The drinks arrive. Maxine's is in an enormous fishbowl of a glass. It's
bright blue, with fruit and marshmallows swimming in it. Paper
umbrellas stick out of it, and plastic monkeys hang from the rim.*

. . . that's the usual?

*Maxine downs it like a shot of whiskey. She pushes the empty glass to
the bartender.*

MAXINE
Set me up again, Barry.

The bartender walks away with the empty glass.

CRAIG
I'm not a homosexual. I just like women for more than their
bodies. Y'know, it's the eternal yin/yang. The male and the
female forces complement each other. One is never complete
without the other. So I absolutely respect that which is
feminine.

MAXINE
You're a fag or a liar.

CRAIG
(*backpedaling*)
I mean, I *am* really attracted to you.

MAXINE
(*mocking*)
I mean, I am *really attracted to you.* Jesus, you *are* a fag. We can share recipes, if you like, Darlene.

Maxine gets up.

CRAIG
(*at a loss*)
No, wait! I like your tits.
(*beat*)
I love your tits. I want to fuck you.

MAXINE
(*sitting*)
Good. Now we're getting somewhere.
(*beat*)
Not a chance.

Maxine's second drink comes. She downs it, pushes the glass toward the bartender.

So, tell me about yourself. If you can get your mind out of the gutter long enough, dog-boy.

CRAIG
Well, I'm a puppeteer . . .

The bartender comes back with Maxine's drink.

MAXINE
(*to bartender*)
Check.

CUT TO:

INT. CRAIG AND LOTTE'S LIVING-ROOM – NIGHT
Lotte is combing Elijah. Craig enters.

CRAIG

Hi.

LOTTE

Hi.

CRAIG
(*nervous, talking too much*)
Sorry I'm so late. Lester just wouldn't let me go. Oh, we're supposed to have dinner with him on Thursday. I can get us out of it if you want. He's really amazing, this insane old lech. It's actually sort of amusing when you get past just how disgusting it is.

There is a silence. Lotte continues to comb out Elijah. Finally:

LOTTE

Did you eat?

CRAIG

Nah. I'm not hungry. I'm sorry I didn't call. It was just, you know, hard to get away.

LOTTE

I was worried.

CRAIG

I'm sorry.
(*trying a joke*)
Hey, you wanted me to work.

There is no reaction from Lotte.

So how was your evening?

LOTTE

Tom-Tom's puncture wound is infected.

CRAIG

The ferret?

LOTTE

The iguana.

CRAIG

Right.

LOTTE

I dressed the wound. Then I've just been feeding everyone, putting everyone to bed.

CRAIG

Yeah. You want a beer?

LOTTE

No thanks. I'm going to turn in.

CRAIG

All right. I'll be in my workshop for a little while. I'll be in in a little while. I need to unwind a little.
(*beat*)
I'll be in soon. A little while.

LOTTE

'kay.

Lotte exits.

CUT TO:

INT. CRAIG AND LOTTE'S STORAGE ROOM – NIGHT

Craig works the Craig and Maxine puppets. The puppets sit on the edge of the small stage and chat. Craig does a pretty fair impersonation of Maxine's voice.

CRAIG
(*as Maxine, fascinated*)
Tell me, Craig, why do you love puppeteering?
(*as Craig*)
Well, Maxine, I'm not sure exactly. Perhaps it's the idea of becoming someone else for a little while. Being inside another skin. Moving differently, thinking differently, feeling differently.
(*as Maxine*)
Interesting. Would you like to be inside my skin, Craig? Think what I think? Feel what I feel?

> (*as Craig*)
More than anything, Maxine.
> (*as Maxine*)
It's good in here, Craig. Better than your wildest dreams.

The puppets kiss.

> CUT TO:

INT. BREAKFAST-ROOM/HALLWAY 7½ FLOOR – DAY

Craig waits at the coffee machine, checks his watch. Finally Maxine approaches.

> CRAIG

Hi.

> MAXINE

You're not someone I could get interested in, Craig. You play with dolls.

> CRAIG
> (*rehearsed*)

Puppets, Maxine. It's the idea of being inside someone else, feeling what they feel, seeing what they see . . .

> MAXINE

Yikes.

Maxine turns to leave.

> CRAIG

Please, let me explain.

Maxine turns back, stares with dead eyes at Craig, waiting.

It's just, and I've never done this before, Maxine, but it's just that I feel something for you. I've never felt this before for anyone, not even my wife. I really believe we belong together, Maxine.

> MAXINE
> (*studies him blankly for a moment*)

How sad it must be for you to be you.

Maxine heads down the hall.

INT. FILE ROOM – DAY

Craig files sadly. When he slams the drawer, some index cards piled on top fall behind the cabinet. He sighs and pushes the cabinet away from the wall to retrieve the cards. He discovers a masonite board nailed to the wall. We can tell it has been there for a long time, because it has been painted over many times. One of the index cards is wedged between the masonite and the wall. Craig reaches for it, but it slips in. He sighs, and begins to pry the board off the wall. Behind the board he discovers a small door.

CRAIG
(facetiously)

Another evil secret of the $7\frac{1}{2}$ floor.

Craig pries open the door. Inside is a dirt tunnel of a maroon, purplish hue.

Holy shit.

For a long moment Craig stares uncomprehendingly into the tunnel, then he picks up a piece of dislodged molding, tentatively reaches into the tunnel, and pokes around. He climbs in.

CUT TO:

INT. TUNNEL – CONTINUOUS

It's dark. Craig crawls along, poking ahead with the molding. As he gets further in, the walls become wet and membranous. There is dripping. The sound of a draft begins. The door slams shut behind him. Suddenly something starts to pull Craig as if he is being sucked through a straw. There is a flash of light.

CUT TO:

INT. FANCY DINING-ROOM – MORNING

The POV of someone reading a newspaper. The person lifts a cup of coffee to his mouth. There is a slurping sound. The person puts down the coffee cup and the newspaper, stands, walks across the room, picks up

*his wallet, and looks in a mirror to checks his teeth for food. It's John
Malkovich. Malkovich walks to the front door, opens it, exits his
apartment.*

                                                    CUT TO:

INT. MAXINE'S OFFICE – CONTINUOUS

*Maxine sits at her desk, eats a sandwich, looks at a fashion magazine,
and chats on the phone.*

                        MAXINE
            The puppeteer told me he loves me today.
                        (laughs)
            I know. I can't think of anything more pathetic.

                                                    CUT TO:

INT. TAXI – CONTINUOUS

*John Malkovich's POV from the back seat of the cab. The cab pulls
away from the curb.*

                        MALKOVICH
                (off-screen, resonant throughout)
            The Broadhurst Theater, please.

The cabbie studies Malkovich in his rear-view mirror as he drives.

                        CABBIE
            Say, aren't you that actor guy?

                        MALKOVICH
                        (off-screen)
            Yeah.

                        CABBIE
            John Makel . . . Mapplethorpe?

                        MALKOVICH
                        (off-screen)
            Malkovich.

                        CABBIE
            Malkovich! Yeah. Hey, I liked you in that one movie.

MALKOVICH
(*off-screen*)

Thank you.

CABBIE

The one where you're that jewel thief.

MALKOVICH
(*off-screen*)

I never played a jewel thief.

CABBIE

Who am I thinking of?

MALKOVICH
(*off-screen*)

I don't know.

CABBIE

I'm pretty sure it was you.

There is a slurping sound. The image starts to fade, then suddenly goes black.

CUT TO:

EXT. DITCH – DAY

It's on the side of Jersey Turnpike. There is a 'pop' and Craig falls from nowhere into the ditch. He is soaking wet, and now dirty from the ditch. He stands, looks confusedly around, sees a New Jersey Turnpike sign. After a moment, he goes to the side of the road and sticks out his thumb.

CUT TO:

INT. MAXINE'S OFFICE – LATER

Maxine sits behind her desk with her feet up, and talks on the phone.

MAXINE

Absolutely, doll. I'm just about to close up here.

Craig walks in, disheveled and exhausted. Maxine sees him, keeps talking.

(*into phone*)
Meet you at The Pig in twenty minutes.
(*laughs lasciviously*)
Oh yeah, *maybe* I'll keep my legs closed till then.
(*hangs up. To Craig*)
I'm splitting for the day. Lock up for me, won't you, darling.

Maxine stands, puts some stuff in her purse.

CRAIG

Don't you want to know what happened to me?

MAXINE
(*considers*)

No.

Maxine heads for the door. Craig grabs her arm.

CRAIG

This is important!

MAXINE
(*looking at his hand on her arm*)

It better be.

Craig lets go of her arm. Maxine lights a cigarette and stands by the open window to smoke it.

CRAIG

There's a tiny door in my office. It's a portal, Maxine. It takes you inside John Malkovich. You see the world through John Malkovich's eyes, then, after about fifteen minutes, you're spit out into a ditch on the side of the New Jersey Turnpike.

MAXINE

Sounds delightful. Who the fuck is John Malkovich?

CRAIG

He's an actor. One of the great American actors of the twentieth century.

MAXINE

What's he been in?

Lots of things. He's very well respected. That jewel thief movie, for example. The point is that this is a very odd thing, *supernatural*, for lack of a better word. It raises all sorts of philosophical questions about the nature of self, about the existence of the soul. Am I me? Is Malkovich Malkovich? Was the Buddha right, is duality an illusion? I had a molding in my hand, Maxine. But I don't have it any more. Where is it? Did it disappear? How could that be? Is it still in Malkovich's head? I don't know! Do you see what a metaphysical can of worms this portal is? I don't think I can go on living my life as I have lived it.

Craig looks pleadingly at Maxine. She gestures toward the open window, then walks out of the room.

CUT TO:

INT. CRAIG AND LOTTE'S LIVING-ROOM – EVENING

Craig slumps blankly on the couch, an untended marionette. The phone rings. He picks it up.

CRAIG

Yeah?

MAXINE
(*phone voice*)
So is this Malkovich fellow appealing?

Maxine has called him at home! He lights up. He paces with the phone.

CRAIG

Yes, of course, Maxine. He's a celebrity.

MAXINE
(*phone voice*)
Good. We'll sell tickets.

CRAIG

Tickets to Malkovich?

MAXINE
(*phone voice*)

Exactly. Two hundred dollars a pop.

CRAIG

But there's something profound here, Maxine, we can't exploit it.

MAXINE
(*phone voice*)

I need you for this, Craig. You're my man on the inside.

The front door opens.

LOTTE
(*off-screen*)

I'm home!

Craig continues the conversation, but in hushed tones.

CRAIG

I'm your man? You need me?

MAXINE
(*phone voice, bored*)

Sure. Whatever.

CRAIG
(*pleased*)

Wow.
(*then, pleadingly*)

But, Maxine, we don't know what the significance of this thing is. It might be very dangerous to toy with.

Lotte walks past Craig into the kitchen with a bag of groceries.

LOTTE

Hey.

Craig waves.

MAXINE
(*phone voice*)

I'll protect you, dollface.

Maxine hangs up.

CRAIG
(*in love, but quietly*)

Oh, Maxine.

DISSOLVE TO:

EXT. CRAIG AND LOTTE'S APARTMENT – NIGHT

Craig and Lotte are in evening clothes and walking to their car.

CRAIG
. . . so I'll have to be working a lot of late nights with my
partner, because my partner and I can't run this business
during the day . . . because LesterCorp is open. But it's a
good thing, Lot, because it's gonna get us out of the hole
financially, so . . .

LOTTE
I don't even understand what you're talking about, Craig.
There is no such thing as a portal into someone else's brain.

CRAIG
Brain, soul, I'm telling you, Lotte, I was right inside him
looking out. You gotta believe me, it's true!

LOTTE
I want to try then.

CRAIG
What?

LOTTE
I want to be John Malkovich. Tomorrow morning. Plus I'd
like to meet this partner of yours.

CRAIG
(*nervously*)
No! Well, you know we can't do it during the day. Like I
explained. I'll tell you what. Let's do it tonight. Right now.

LOTTE
Now?

CRAIG

Yeah. We'll do it right now. On the way to Lester's house.

CUT TO:

INT. FILE ROOM – NIGHT

Craig holds open the small door as Lotte hesitantly climbs in.

CRAIG

I'll meet you by the side of the road on the New Jersey turnpike.

LOTTE

I'm scared.

CRAIG

I know. You don't have to do this.

LOTTE
(*kidlike*)

No, I will.

She crawls out of view. Craig hurries from the office.

CUT TO:

INT. BATHROOM – NIGHT

Malkovich is in the shower. We watch from his POV as he soaps himself. He does this in a sensual manner.

LOTTE
(*voice-over*)

Oh, wet. Wet. Weird.

Malkovich steps out of the shower, slowly towels himself dry.

Ooh, that's nice. Oh. Yes.

Malkovich looks at himself in the mirror.

I feel sexy.

CUT TO:

EXT. DITCH – NIGHT

Craig stands in the foreground watching the ditch, waiting. His car is in the background, headlights pointing in the direction Craig is looking. Lotte lands in the ditch behind Craig. He turns to see. She is wet and ragged and walking determinedly toward the car. Craig hurries to catch up.

> LOTTE
>
> I have to go back.

> CRAIG
>
> Okay. Maybe tomorrow.

> LOTTE
>
> I have to go back *now*.

Lotte gets into the passenger seat, closes her door, stares straight ahead.

> CRAIG
>
> We'll talk about it later.

CUT TO:

INT. CRAIG AND LOTTE'S CAR/TURNPIKE – NIGHT

Craig drives. Lotte looks distractedly out the window.

> LOTTE
>
> I have to go back, Craig. Being inside did something to me. All of a sudden everything made sense. I knew who I was.

> CRAIG
>
> You weren't you. You were John Malkovich.

> LOTTE
> (*tickled*)
>
> I was, wasn't I?
> (*yelling out the window*)
> I was John *fucking* Malkovich!
> (*laughs, then intensely*)
> Take me back, Craig.

> CRAIG
>
> We're late for Lester.

INT. LESTER'S DINING-ROOM – NIGHT

It's a posh place with flocked wallpaper and candelabras. Lester, Craig, and Lotte sit around an elegantly appointed table with all different sorts of juices in front of them. Lotte is still wet, still distracted. Lester sits quite close to her.

> LESTER
> Tell me, Lotte, can you understand a word I'm saying?

> LOTTE
> *(hesitates, then:)*
> Yes, of course, Dr Lester. You were explaining the nutritional value of ingesting minerals in a colloidal form. And I really couldn't agree more!

> LESTER
> Oh, be still my heart.

An unhappy Craig sips one of the juices before him.

> LOTTE
> Dr Lester, would you point me toward the restroom?

> LESTER
> With immense pleasure, my dear. Go up the grand *escalier*. Once atop the stairhead, you'll want to enter the . . .
> *(calculates silently)*
> . . . fifth door on *my* left. Now be sure to watch the step down. It's sunken, you know.

Lotte smiles. Lester returns the smile. Lotte heads down the hall.

> *(to Craig)*
> More beet-spinach juice, my friend?

CUT TO:

INT. LESTER'S STAIRWAY – NIGHT

Lotte climbs the magnificent staircase. At the top she finds six closed doors. She counts, trying to make sense of Lester's instructions. Finally she opens one of the doors, looks inside, gasps.

INT. LESTER'S ROOM – CONTINUOUS

Lotte enters the room. It is dimly lit. The walls are covered with photographs of John Malkovich. It looks like a museum: photos of Malkovich as a boy, as a young man, mug-shot-style profiles, life-sized naked photos of Malkovich from various angles, photocopies of official documents: birth certificate, college diploma, handwriting samples, a family tree.

> LOTTE
> (*under breath*)

What the hell . . . ?

CUT TO:

INT. CRAIG AND LOTTE'S CAR/BRIDGE – NIGHT

Craig and Lotte drive home.

> LOTTE

What do you suppose Lester's relationship with John Malkovich is?

> CRAIG

That portal's been boarded up for ever. I bet Lester's not even aware of it. Why?

> LOTTE

No reason. I was just thinking, do you think it's weird that John Malkovich has a portal? Do you think it might have some . . . *significance*, for example?

> CRAIG

What the hell kind of question is that?

> LOTTE

I don't know.
> (*beat, attitude shift*)

It's sort of sexy that he has a portal though, don't you think? Y'know, it's almost . . . vaginal. It's like he's got a penis and a vagina. It's sort of like Malkovich's feminine side. I like that.

Craig considers this.

CUT TO:

INT. CRAIG AND LOTTE'S STORAGE ROOM – NIGHT

Craig sits at his work table. We hear the shower running in the background. Craig is pulling the heads off of the Craig and the Maxine puppets. He puts the Maxine head on the Craig puppet. He puts the Craig head on the Maxine puppet. He sighs.

CRAIG

My kingdom for *your* portal, Maxine.

CUT TO:

INT. CRAIG AND LOTTE'S BATHROOM – NIGHT

Lotte, in the shower, turns it off and steps out. She towels herself dry in much the same way as Malkovich. Her eyes are closed. She opens them slowly and sees herself in the mirror. Disappointedly, she drops the towel and heads out of the bathroom.

CUT TO:

INT. MAXINE'S OFFICE – MORNING

The door is ajar. Maxine sits at her desk composing an ad. Craig stands behind her, ostensibly looking over her shoulder, but actually studying the back of her head. Gently he tries to move her hair to view the back of her head. She shoos him away like a bug. He sighs.

CUT TO:

INT. ELEVATOR – CONTINUOUS

Lotte is in the elevator as it ascends. She holds the crowbar. A few old people ride up with her. She smiles at them. They smile back.

CUT TO:

INT. MAXINE'S OFFICE – CONTINUOUS

> MAXINE

Okay. Here it is.

> *(reading)*

'Ever want to be someone else? Now you can. No kidding. Only two hundred dollars for fifteen minutes. Visit J.M. Inc., Mertin-Flemmer Building, nightly from 9 p.m. to 4 a.m.'

> CRAIG

Sounds good. Oblique but intriguing. Phone it in.

Maxine dials the phone. Lotte peeks in.

> CRAIG
> *(What is she doing here?)*

Lotte!

> LOTTE

I heard your voice.

> *(to Maxine)*

Hello.

> CRAIG

Why aren't you at work?

> LOTTE

Is this your partner? She's pretty. I had to come back and do the Malkovich ride again. Fuck everything else. Is this her?

> MAXINE
> *(into phone)*

Yes, hello, I wanted to place an ad.

> *(to Lotte)*

Hi, you're Craig's wife?

> LOTTE

Yes. Hi.

> CRAIG

Lotte, Maxine. Maxine, Lotte.

Lotte and Maxine shake hands.

LOTTE

Hi. Have you done Malkovich yet?

MAXINE

Hi, uh . . .

(*into phone*)

Hi. I wanted to place an ad. Yes. '*Ever want to be someone else?*' No, that's the ad, but let's talk about you in a minute. '*Ever want to be someone else? Now you can. No kidding . . .*'

CRAIG

(*to Lotte*)

You should be at work.

LOTTE

I've been going over and over my experience last night. It was amazing.

(*beat*)

I've decided I'm a transsexual. Isn't that the craziest thing?

CRAIG

What, are you nuts?

LOTTE

Everything felt right for the first time. I need to go back to make sure, then if the feeling is still there, I'm going to speak to Dr Feldman about sexual reassignment surgery.

CRAIG

This is absurd. Besides, Feldman's an allergist. If you're going to do something, do it right.

Lotte starts to tear up. This works on Craig, but he fights against it and continues his attack.

Y'know, it's just that you get these ideas and then you do a half-assed job.

LOTTE

I like Dr Feldman, okay? So I thought I'd ask him for his advice. Is that so terrible? Why do you always have to yell at me like this?

CRAIG
(*feeling bad*)

It's only the thrill of seeing through someone else's eyes, sweetie. It'll pass.

LOTTE

Don't stand in the way of my actualization as a man, Craig.

Craig tries to respond to this, but can't.

MAXINE
(*hanging up the phone*)

Let her go, Craig.
(*smiling at Lotte*)

I mean 'him'.

CRAIG
(*anything for Maxine*)

Yeah, okay.
(*a thought*)

But it's the middle of the day. How am I going to get her past Lester?

MAXINE

Yawn. Figure it out.

Craig sighs and leads Lotte out of the office. Maxine dials the phone.

(*into phone*)

Davey? Max. Get me John Malkovich's home phone? That's great. Love ya and owe ya.

CUT TO:

INT. JOHN MALKOVICH'S LIVING-ROOM – DAY

Malkovich's POV. He sits on the couch, drinks coffee, and reads a copy of The Cherry Orchard. *Bach plays on the stereo in the background.*

MALKOVICH
(*reading aloud*)

'I am hungry as the winter; I am sick, anxious, poor as a beggar. Fate has tossed me hither and thither; I have been everywhere, everywhere.'

LOTTE
(*voice-over*)

What raw, animal power!

MALKOVICH

'But wherever I have been, every minute, day and night, my soul has been full of mysterious anticipations.'

The phone rings. Malkovich puts down the script, and picks up the phone.

(*into phone*)

Yeah?

MAXINE
(*off-screen, phone voice*)

Mr Malkovich?

MALKOVICH

Who's calling?

MAXINE
(*phone-voice*)

You don't know me, but I'm a great admirer of yours.

MALKOVICH

How'd you get this number?

MAXINE
(*phone voice*)

It's just that I fantasize about you, and, well, speaking to you now has gotten me sort of excited and . . .

LOTTE
(*voice-over, turned on*)

Oh, I like this.

MALKOVICH

Listen, this is not amusing. Please don't call here any . . .

MAXINE
(*phone voice, giggling*)

Ooh, such authority! My nipples are at attention, General Malkovich, *sir*. So I'll be at Bernardo's tonight at eight.

Please, please meet me there. I just adored you in that jewel-thief movie . . .

Malkovich hangs up the phone.

> LOTTE
> (*voice-over*)

My God!

> (*attempting thought control*)

Meet her there. Meet her there. Meet her there. Meet her there. Meet her there . . .

Malkovich goes back to his script.

Meet her there. Meet her there. Meet her there . . .

Malkovich picks up a pen and writes: Bernardo's 8.00.

CUT TO:

EXT. DITCH – MORNING

Craig waits. Lotte pops into the ditch. She's wet and slimy.

> CRAIG

How was it?

> LOTTE

I have to go back tonight. At eight. Exactly.

> CRAIG

Why?

> LOTTE

Don't crowd me, Craig.

CUT TO:

INT. BERNARDO'S – NIGHT

Malkovich's POV. It's a busy Italian restaurant. Malkovich looks around, checks his watch: 8.03. A guy walks up to him.

> GUY

Excuse me, are you John Malkovich?

MALKOVICH

Yes.

GUY

Wow. You were really great in that movie where you played that retard.

MALKOVICH

Thank you very much.

GUY

I just wanted to tell you that. And say thank you. I have a cousin that's a retard, so, as you can imagine, it means a lot to me to see retards portrayed on the silver screen so compassionately.

The guy walks away. Malkovich scans the room. Maxine enters the restaurant. We see her, but Malkovich doesn't single her out of the crowd. She looks around.

LOTTE
(*voice-over*)

Maxine!

Maxine spots Malkovich, and heads over. He focuses on her.

MAXINE

Hi. I'm so glad you decided to come. I'm Maxine.

Maxine holds out her hand. She is charming. Malkovich takes her hand.

MALKOVICH

I'm John. I didn't think I was going to come, but I felt oddly compelled. I have to admit I was a bit intrigued by your voice.

LOTTE
(*voice-over*)

God, she's beautiful. The way she's looking at me. At him. At us.

MAXINE

And the funny thing is, Mr Malkovich, my voice is probably the least intriguing thing about me.

LOTTE
(*voice-over*)
I've never been looked at like this by a woman.

MALKOVICH
Can I get you a drink?

MAXINE
Whatever you're having.

CUT TO:

INT. CRAIG AND LOTTE'S CAR/TURNPIKE – NIGHT

Craig drives. Lotte is soaking wet. She stares out the window.

CRAIG
So how was it? What was he doing?

LOTTE
Oh, you know, not a lot. Just hanging around his apartment. I think he must be a lonely man.

CRAIG
You see, men can feel unfulfilled, too. I'm glad you're realizing that. You shouldn't be so quick to assume that switching bodies would be the answer to all your problems.

LOTTE
You're right. You know I was thinking that we should have Maxine over for dinner. Since you two are partners and all. It might be a nice gesture.

CRAIG
I don't know. There's some tension between us. I'd hate to expose you to that.

LOTTE
It'll be okay. I'll fix my lasagne. We'll smoke a joint.
(*dreamily*)
Tensions will melt away.

CUT TO:

INT. CRAIG AND LOTTE'S DINING-ROOM – NIGHT

*Craig, Lotte and Maxine are seated at the table and eating lasagne.
Lotte eyes Maxine. Craig eyes Maxine. There is an awkward silence.*

> **LOTTE**
> (*to Maxine*)
>
> Did you know that Eskimos have not one, but forty-nine
> words for snow. It's because they have so much of it. So
> much snow.

> **CRAIG**
>
> After dinner I'll show you my puppets.

> **MAXINE**
>
> Ah.

> **LOTTE**
>
> After that I'll introduce you to my favorite monkey, Elijah.
> He's got an ulcer, due to a suppressed childhood trauma. But
> we're getting to the bottom of it.
> (*whispers*)
> Psychotherapy.

> > > **CUT TO:**

INT. CRAIG AND LOTTE'S LIVING-ROOM – A BIT LATER

*Dinner is over. Craig, Maxine and Lotte sit on the couch passing a joint
back and forth. They are stoned.*

> **MAXINE**
> (*to no one in particular*)
>
> The way I see it, the world is divided into those who go after
> what they want and those who don't. The passionate ones,
> the ones who go after what they want may not get what they
> want, but they remain vital, in touch with themselves, and
> when they lie on their deathbeds, they have few regrets. The
> ones who don't go after what they want . . . well, who gives a
> shit about them anyway?

*Maxine laughs. There is another silence. Suddenly, at the same
moment, both Craig and Lotte lunge for Maxine and start kissing her*

passionately about the face and neck. They stop just as suddenly and look at each other.

> ### CRAIG
>
> You?

Lotte looks away.

> ### MAXINE
>
> Craig, I just don't find you attractive. And, Lotte, I'm smitten with you, but only when you're in Malkovich. When I looked into his eyes last night, I could feel you peering out. Behind the stubble and the too-prominent brow and the male pattern baldness, I sensed your feminine longing, and it just slew me.

> ### CRAIG
> *(disgusted)*
>
> My God.

Lotte strokes Maxine's face. Craig gets up, stares out window.

> ### MAXINE
> *(to Lotte, removing her hand)*
> Only as *John*, sweetie. I'm sorry.
> *(gets up)*
> Thanks for a wonderful dinner.
> *(walks past window. To Craig)*
> No hard feelings, partner.

Maxine exits. Craig and Lotte look at each other, really stoned, trying to focus on the grave situation.

> ### LOTTE
>
> I want a divorce.

CUT TO:

INT. HALLWAY, 7½ FLOOR/RECEPTION – NIGHT

The hallway is empty with only the exit signs illuminating it. The door to LesterCorp is propped open and a sign reading 'J.M. Inc.' is taped to it.

CUT TO:

52

INT. FILE ROOM – NIGHT

It is deadly silent. Craig and Maxine sit on folding chairs. The wall clock ticks. Craig whistles tunelessly, every once in a while looking up and discreetly checking out Maxine. Eventually there is a knock at the door.

CRAIG
(*a little too urgently*)

Come in!

Erroll, a sad, fat young man, enters meekly.

ERROLL

Hello. I'm here about the ad.

CRAIG

Please, have a seat.

Erroll sits in a chair in front of Craig. He glances nervously over at Maxine.

ERROLL

When you say, I can be somebody else, what do you mean exactly?

CRAIG

Exactly that. We can put you inside someone else's body for fifteen minutes.

ERROLL

Oh, this is just the medical breakthrough I've been waiting for. Are there side effects? Please say no! Please say no! Please say no!

MAXINE

No.

ERROLL

Long-term psychic or physiological repercussions?

MAXINE

Don't be an ass.

ERROLL

Can I be anyone I want?

CRAIG

Well . . .

MAXINE

You can be John Malkovich.

ERROLL

That's perfect! My second choice. Ah, this is wonderful. Too good to be true! You see, I'm a sad man. Sad and fat and alone. Oh, I've tried all the diets, my friends. Lived for a year on nothing but imitation mayonnaise. Did it work? You be the judge. But Malkovich! King of New York! Man about town! Most eligible bachelor! *Bon viveur*! The Schopenhauer of the twentieth century! Thin man extraordinaire!

MAXINE

Two hundred dollars.

ERROLL

Yes. Yes. A thousand times, yes!

Erroll hands Maxine the cash and is ushered into the portal. The door slams closed.

CUT TO:

INT. JOHN MALKOVICH'S KITCHEN – NIGHT

We see through Malkovich's eyes as he studies a mail-order catalogue and talks on the phone.

MALKOVICH

. . . and I don't need a bath mat, so if I get the set, can I substitute three extra hand towels for the bath mat?

TELEPHONE VOICE

Yes, sir. Sure, we can do that.

MALKOVICH

Okay, good. So I'll take the periwinkle.

TELEPHONE VOICE

Oh, I'm sorry. We're out of stock in periwinkle. Do you want to back-order?

MALKOVICH

That's okay. I should probably go with the loden anyway.

CUT TO:

EXT. DITCH – NIGHT

Craig waits by his car, checks his watch. Pop! Erroll plops into the ditch, wet and unkempt. He looks around, sees Craig, charges him with a yell and gives him an enormous bear hug.

ERROLL

Oh, thank you! Thank you! A thousand times, thank you!

CRAIG
(*gasping for air*)

Tell your friends.

ERROLL

Oh, I will, I will! and I know many people who would love this service. I know many people who are sad and alone and would love a chance to be someone good. Most of them with John Malkovich as their second choice!

CUT TO:

INT. CRAIG AND LOTTE'S LIVING-ROOM – LATE AFTERNOON

Craig lies listlessly on his back on the floor and stares at the ceiling. Lotte enters with a bag of groceries.

LOTTE

Hey.

CRAIG

Hey.

Lotte puts the groceries down, falls back onto the couch. A cat jumps on to her lap. She absently strokes it as she watches Craig for a bit.

LOTTE
Boy, she's really done a number on us, huh?

CRAIG
Yeah.

LOTTE
It's like somehow when she first looked at me, my whole life before that moment became irrelevant.

CRAIG
I know what you mean.

LOTTE
Did we ever love each other like we love her, Craig?

CRAIG
I can't remember.

LOTTE
I don't think we did.

CRAIG
I don't think so.

LOTTE
(*beat*)
She doesn't love either of us, you know.

CRAIG
So it seems.

He and Lotte stare at each other for a long while.

LOTTE
Can't we teach ourselves to love each other the way we love her?

CRAIG
It would seem the practical thing to do, wouldn't it?

Lotte lies on her back on the floor next to Craig. They both stare at the ceiling.

LOTTE
We've put so much time into this relationship after all.

CRAIG

We really have.

LOTTE

I have a great deal of affection for you, Craig.

CRAIG

I know. Me too.

Lotte turns and kisses Craig on the cheek.

What about Maxine?

LOTTE

Fuck Maxine.

CRAIG

We wish.

They look at each other and laugh, then fall into an embrace. They begin to make love, both clearly somewhere else.

DISSOLVE TO:

INT. CRAIG AND LOTTE'S BEDROOM – LATER

Craig and Lotte are in bed. Craig is asleep. Lotte's eyes are open. She quietly gets out of bed.

CUT TO:

INT. FILE ROOM – NIGHT

The phone rings. Maxine is being given a bikini wax by an attractive, uniformed young woman.

MAXINE

J.M. Inc.

LOTTE
(phone voice, whispering)
I have to see you. Please. Can you call him and invite yourself over.

MAXINE

Um, when?

LOTTE
(*phone voice*)
Give me one hour to get inside. Exactly. Thank you, Maxine.

Maxine checks the watch on the uniformed woman's wrist, which is busily at work in Maxine's crotch. The time is 3.11 a.m.

CUT TO:

INT. MALKOVICH'S APARTMENT – A BIT LATER

The doorbell rings. Malkovich answers it. Maxine stands there in a sheer black nightgown.

MAXINE
Thanks so much for having me over, sugar plum.

MALKOVICH
Oh, I'm really glad you called.

Malkovich starts to grope Maxine.

Shall we to the boudoir?

She lifts his hand from her crotch and checks his wristwatch. The time is 4.05.

MAXINE
Couple a minutes. I'm early.

CUT TO:

INT. MALKOVICH'S LIVING-ROOM – NIGHT

Maxine and Malkovich sit a bit awkwardly next to each other on the couch.

MAXINE
So, do you enjoy being an actor?

MALKOVICH
Oh sure. It's very rewarding . . .

The digital clock on the VCR clicks over to 4.11 a.m. Maxine's look softens, and she kisses Malkovich hard on the lips. He seems surprised,

58

but quickly warms to it. We shift to Malkovich's POV as Maxine begins to unbutton Malkovich's shirt.

> LOTTE
> (*voice-over*)
> Oh my darling. Oh my sweetheart.

> MAXINE
> I love you, Lotte.

> LOTTE
> (*voice-over*)
> Maxine . . .

> MALKOVICH
> (*stopping*)
> I'm sorry, did you just call me 'Lotte'?

> MAXINE
> Do you mind?

> MALKOVICH
> (*thinking*)
> No, I guess not.

They go back to it.

> MAXINE
> Oh, my sweet, beautiful Lotte.

> MALKOVICH
> (*thinks he's playing along*)
> Yes, Maxine, yes.

> LOTTE
> (*voice-over*)
> This is so right.

CUT TO:

EXT. DITCH – NIGHT

With a gasp and a wail of release, Lotte pops into the ditch. She is soaking wet and breathes heavily. She just lies there.

CUT TO:

INT. CRAIG AND LOTTE'S KITCHEN – EARLY MORNING

Craig sits hunched over a cup of coffee. The front door is heard opening. After a moment Lotte appears in the kitchen doorway. She is caked with dirt. Craig looks up at her.

                    CRAIG
You were *him*, weren't you?

                    LOTTE
                    (*quietly*)
Yes.

                    CRAIG
And he was with her.

                    LOTTE
We love her, Craig. I'm sorry.

                    CRAIG
We?

                    LOTTE
Me and John.

                    CRAIG
Don't forget me.

                    LOTTE
Well, you have the Maxine action figure to play with.

Craig looks down at his coffee.

I'm sorry. That was nasty.

                    CRAIG
Life is confusing, isn't it?

                    LOTTE
Jesus. Who knew?

                    CRAIG
I feel that my parents never prepared me to deal with this situation. But I guess, y'know, today's world is so much more complicated than theirs.

60

(beat)
I have to move out for a while, Lot. Living here is too painful.

LOTTE
I'm so sorry, Craig.

CUT TO:

INT. LESTERCORP WORK AREA – MORNING

Craig looks sadly out the window while an oblivious Floris happily jabbers away at him.

CUT TO:

INT. FILE ROOM – NIGHT

Craig enters with red-rimmed eyes. Maxine sits on the floor and leans against a cabinet. She's wearing a short skirt, her legs are casually spread and she appears radiant.

MAXINE
You're late, my little cowboy.

CRAIG
Are you torturing me on purpose?

MAXINE
(matter of fact)
I've fallen in love.

CRAIG
I don't think so. I've fallen in love! *This* is what people who've fallen in love look like!

MAXINE
You picked the unrequited variety. Very bad for the skin.

CRAIG
You're evil, Maxine.

MAXINE
Do you have any idea what it's like to have two people look at you with total lust and devotion through the same pair of eyes? No, I don't suppose you would. It's quite a thrill, Craiggy.

Craig turns and walks out the door.

CUT TO:

INT. HALLWAY 7½ FLOOR – CONTINUOUS

Craig hurries past a long line of empty-looking people, all clutching cash. His face is red with rage.

CUT TO:

INT. CRAIG AND LOTTE'S LIVING-ROOM – NIGHT

Craig stands still and tense, with gun in hand. We hear the front door unlock. Lotte enters. She does not see Craig. He grabs her from behind as she passes. Lotte screams. Craig holds the gun to her head.

LOTTE
What the hell you are doing? Jesus, is that real?

CRAIG
It's real and I don't know how to use it very well, so don't make any sudden moves.

LOTTE
Craig, I'm your goddamn wife and you're holding a gun to my head?

CRAIG
Yeah, well, maybe if you acted like a woman –

LOTTE
Suck my dick!

Craig shoves Lotte. She falls. She looks up, stunned by this. Craig looks stunned by what he did, too.

CRAIG
(*almost apologetically*)
Shut up, okay?

Keeping the gun trained on Lotte, Craig dials the phone. He hands the receiver to her. He holds his ear close to the receiver also.

Tell her you need to see her.

                    LOTTE
                   (*to Craig*)
You bastard.

Craig cocks the pistol.

                    MAXINE
                 (*phone voice*)
J.M. Inc. Be all that someone else can be.

                    LOTTE
                (*looking at Craig*)
I have to see you.

                    MAXINE
                 (*phone voice*)
Sweetie! Oh, but we can't. It's business hours. I need to keep
the membranous tunnel open for paying customers.

                    CRAIG
                   (*sotto*)
Tell her, what the hell, close early tonight, live dangerously.

                    LOTTE
What the hell. Close early tonight, live dangerously.

                    MAXINE
                 (*phone voice*)
Oooh, doll. I love this new devil-may-care side of you.
Alrighty, I'll track down lover-boy, and I'll see both of you in
one hour. Exactamundo.

*Maxine hangs up. Lotte hands the phone to Craig, who hangs it up.
Craig opens up the big cage where Elijah is housed, and motions with
the gun for Lotte to enter.*

                    LOTTE
                  (*screaming*)
Help! He's locking me in a cage!

Craig shakes her from behind. She looks at him sadly.

NEIGHBOR
(*phone voice*)
Shut that damn parrot up!

PARROT
Shut up! Shut up!

CRAIG
Sorry!

Without making eye contact, Craig tapes Lotte's mouth and ties her hands and feet. Elijah watches him tie her. He becomes somewhat agitated, and holds his stomach.

CUT TO:

INT. BROADHURST THEATER – NIGHT

Malkovich is dressed as Richard III, complete with hump. He is rehearsing some business on-stage. Maxine watches from the house.

MALKOVICH
(*as Richard*)
Was ever woman in this humour woo'd?
Was ever woman in this humour won?

Maxine anxiously checks her watch, then points to it so Malkovich can see.

MALKOVICH
Tommy, can I take fifteen?

CUT TO:

INT. MALKOVICH'S DRESSING-ROOM – NIGHT

Malkovich and Maxine are having sex on the make-up table, against the mirror.

MAXINE
Oh, Lotte . . . Oh, sweetie . . .

We now watch the scene from Malkovich's POV.

MALKOVICH

Maxine . . .

CRAIG
(*voice-over*)
I can't believe it. This is too good to be true.

CUT TO:

INT. FILE ROOM – NIGHT

Craig is toweling himself off, hurriedly combing his hair. Maxine enters.

CRAIG
You're glowing again.

MAXINE
A girl has a right to glow if she wants. It's in the fucking constitution.

Maxine sits. Craig smiles to himself.

CUT TO:

INT. CRAIG AND LOTTE'S LIVING-ROOM – EVENING

Craig is feeding the various caged animals. He puts two plates of food in Elijah's cage. Lotte is ungagged and unbound now. He talks as he works.

CRAIG
(*earnest and excited*)
It was really really great being you being Malkovich, Lot. I'd never seen the passionate side of Maxine before, or her breasts for that matter. Geez, I really wish you could've been there.
(*beat*)
So I've been thinking to myself, if only I could actually feel what Malkovich feels, rather than just see what he sees . . . And then, if only I could control his arms, his legs, his pelvis, and make them work for me. Y'know?

LOTTE
It'll never happen, fuckface.

Craig is startled, taken aback by Lotte's intense anger. He hesitates, then responds neutrally:

> CRAIG

It'll happen, Lotte. It's what I do. I'm a puppeteer.

Craig picks up the phone and dials. He holds the receiver up to Lotte's face.

CUT TO:

INT. MAXINE'S APARTMENT – DAWN

Malkovich and Maxine are having sex on Maxine's couch.

> MAXINE

Lotte, this is so good . . .

> CRAIG
> (*voice-over, tense, commanding*)

Move right hand across her left breast now. Move right hand across her left breast now. Move right hand across her left breast now.

Malkovich clumsily, awkwardly moves his hand across Maxine's breast.

Holy shit, yes!

> MALKOVICH

Howa shit! Yes!

> CRAIG
> (*voice-over*)

Holy shit! He said what I said!

> MALKOVICH

Howa shit! He said wha I said!

> MAXINE

Lotte? Is that you?

> CRAIG
> (*voice-over*)

Yes, yes, sweetheart, yes!

Yes, yes, swee'heart, yes!
>(scared)
What the fuck is going on? I'm not talking. This is not me!

MAXINE

Oh, Lotte . . .

Maxine kisses Malkovich hard on the lips. There is a sucking sound.

CUT TO:

EXT. DITCH – DAWN

There is a pop and Craig lands in the ditch.

CUT TO:

INT. MAXINE'S APARTMENT – DAWN

A panicked Malkovich is pulling on his clothes.

MALKOVICH

Something was making me talk. Some goddamn thing was making me move. I gotta get out of here.

MAXINE

Oh, dollface, it was just your passion for me taking hold.

MALKOVICH

No, *dollface*, I know what my passion taking hold feels like. I gotta go.

He leaves. Maxine falls back on the couch and sighs contentedly.

CUT TO:

INT. CRAIG AND LOTTE'S LIVING-ROOM – EARLY MORNING

The front door opens. A wet, messy Craig hurries into the room and past Lotte's cage. Lotte is bound and gagged. Craig is pulling off his wet clothes, and throwing on clean clothes.

CRAIG

I did it, sweetie. I moved his arm across your girlfriend's

glorious tit. I made him talk, sort of. And, oh, there was the beginning of sensation in the fingertips. Ummmm-mmmm! It's just a matter of practice before Malkovich becomes nothing more than another one of my puppets.

Dressed, Craig dashes out of the apartment.

CUT TO:

EXT. CITY STREET – EARLY MORNING

Craig hurries toward the Mertin-Flemmer building.

CUT TO:

INT. HALLWAY, $7\frac{1}{2}$ FLOOR/RECEPTION – EARLY MORNING

Craig is unlocking the door to LesterCorp. The elevator doors are heard to open and close. Lester turns the corner, sees Craig.

LESTER

Schwartz!

CRAIG

Good morning, sir!

Craig gets the door unlocked and hurries in.

CUT TO:

INT. LESTERCORP RECEPTION AREA – CONTINUOUS

Craig runs through.

CUT TO:

INT. LESTERCORP WORK AREA – CONTINUOUS

Craig weaves past many computer terminals in the empty room.

CUT TO:

INT. FILE ROOM – CONTINUOUS

Craig hurries into the room, ripping the paper J.M. Inc. sign from the door, crumpling it and tossing it in the garbage can. He struggles to shove the heavy file cabinet back against the portal door. He's sweating as he anxiously scans the room for other telltale signs. He spots a big photo of Malkovich tacked to the wall just as Lester enters.

LESTER
Schwartz, you're in a hurry this morning.

CRAIG
I just wanted to get an early start on my day.

LESTER
I like a dedicated worker. A dedicated worker is a worker who goes places at LesterCorp.

Lester indicates the direction 'up'. Craig nods appreciatively, tries not to glance at the photo of Malkovich behind Lester's head.

So how's that wife of yours? She's a corker.

CRAIG
Lotte's fine, sir.

LESTER
You're a lucky man to have a wife who's pretty and interested in nutrition, Schwartz.

CRAIG
I know, sir. That's very true.

They nod at each other for a while.

LESTER
So, what's new?

CUT TO:

INT. MALKOVICH'S APARTMENT – EARLY MORNING

The shades are drawn. Malkovich paces nervously, a glass of whiskey in his hand. Charlie Sheen sits on the couch and fiddles with a Rubik's Cube. He occasionally sips from a blue paper cup of Greek diner coffee.

MALKOVICH
It's like nothing I've ever felt before. I think I'm going crazy.

CHARLIE SHEEN
I'm sure you're not going crazy.

MALKOVICH
Charlie, I'm telling you . . . it was like nothing I've . . .

CHARLIE SHEEN
Yeah yeah yeah. Yadda yadda yadda. Were you stoned?

MALKOVICH
Yes, but you see, someone else was talking through my mouth . . .

CHARLIE SHEEN
You were stoned. Case closed. End of story. How hot is this babe?

MALKOVICH
I think it might've been this Lotte woman talking through me. Maxine likes to call me Lotte.

CHARLIE SHEEN
Ouch. Now that's hot. She's using you to channel some dead lesbian lover. Let me know when you're done with her. This is my type of chick.

MALKOVICH
I'm done with her now. Tonight really creeped me out.

CHARLIE SHEEN
You're crazy to let go of a chick who calls you Lotte. I tell you that as a friend.

MALKOVICH
I don't know anything about her. What if she's some kind of witch or something?

CHARLIE SHEEN
All the better. Hey, Hot Lesbian Witches. That's genius!

MALKOVICH
I gotta know the truth, Charlie.

CHARLIE SHEEN
Truth is for suckers, Johnny-boy.

CUT TO:

EXT. APARTMENT BUILDING – NIGHT

Malkovich, in a baseball cap and sunglasses, sits in a parked car. He drinks from a thermos. After a moment, Maxine emerges from the building and hails a cab. Malkovich follows at a safe distance.

CUT TO:

INT. $7\frac{1}{2}$ FLOOR – NIGHT

The elevator doors are pried open. It's packed with sad people. Maxine and the sad people climb out. The last to emerge is Malkovich. He is astounded by the squat dimensions of the floor. He turns the corner and sees a long line of crouching depressed-looking people. Maxine goes into the office and closes the door. Malkovich sees 'J.M. Inc.' taped to the door. He turns to the first man in line.

MALKOVICH
Excuse me, what type of service does this company provide?

SAD MAN
You get to be John Malkovich for fifteen minutes. Two hundred clams.

MALKOVICH
(*quietly flipped*)
I see.

SAD MAN
No cutting, by the way.

Malkovich pounds on the door.

No cutting!

Several people jump on Malkovich, and start beating him. Craig steps out of the office.

CRAIG
Hey! Break it up! Break it up! Everybody gets a chance to be . . .

The people climb off Malkovich. His glasses and cap have been knocked off and everyone recognizes him.

> SAD MAN
>
> It's him! Oh, I'm so sorry, Mr Malkovich! I hope we didn't hurt you too terribly. It's such a thrill to meet you.

> MALKOVICH
> (*to Craig*)
>
> Inside.

CUT TO:

INT. FILE ROOM – CONTINUOUS

Craig and Malkovich enter. Maxine looks up, startled, but controlling it.

> MAXINE
>
> Darling!

> MALKOVICH
>
> What the fuck is going on?

> CRAIG
>
> Mr Malkovich, my name is Craig Schwartz. I can explain. We operate a little business here that . . . simulates, for our clientele, the experience of . . . being you, actually.

> MALKOVICH
>
> Simulates?

> CRAIG
>
> Sure, after a fashion.

> MALKOVICH
>
> What exactly is it like?

> CRAIG
>
> Well, it's hard to describe exactly –

> MALKOVICH
>
> I want to try then.

CRAIG

You? Why, I'm sure it would pale in comparison to the actual experience.

MALKOVICH

Let me try!

CRAIG

Yes, but right now Mr Hiroshi is in the –

MAXINE

Let him try.

CRAIG

Of course, right this way, Mr Malkovich. Compliments of the house.

Craig ushers Malkovich to the portal door, opens it.

MALKOVICH

Jesus.

Malkovich climbs in. The door closes.

CRAIG

What happens when a man climbs through his own portal?

MAXINE
(goes back to magazine)

Oh, who cares?

CUT TO:

INT. MEMBRANOUS TUNNEL – NIGHT

Malkovich crawls through for a long time. It's murky. He's getting more and more frightened. Suddenly there is a slurping sound and Malkovich is pulled through a blindingly white nothingness.

CUT TO:

INT. RESTAURANT – NIGHT

Malkovich pops into a chair in a swank night-club. He's wearing a tuxedo. The woman across the table from him is also Malkovich, but in

73

a gown. He looks around the restaurant. Everyone is Malkovich in different clothes. Malkovich is panicked. The girl Malkovich across the table looks at him seductively, winks and talks.

> GIRL MALKOVICH
> Malkovich Malkovich Malkovich Malkovich . . .

Malkovich looks confused. The Malkovich Waiter approaches, pen and pad in hand, ready to take their orders.

> WAITER MALKOVICH
> Malkovich Malkovich Malkovich?

> GIRL MALKOVICH
> (*studying menu*)
> Malkovich Malkovich Malkovich Malkovich.

> WAITER MALKOVICH
> Malkovich Malkovich.
> (*turning to Malkovich*)
> Malkovich?

Malkovich looks down at the men. Every item is 'Malkovich'. He screams:

> MALKOVICH
> Malkovich!

The waiter jots it down on his pad.

> WAITER MALKOVICH
> Malkovich.

Malkovich pushes himself away from the table and runs for the exit. He passes the stage where a girl singer Malkovich is singing sensuously into the microphone. She is backed by a forties-style big band of Malkoviches.

> SINGING MALKOVICH
> Malkovich Malkovich Malkovich Malkovich . . .

Malkovich flies through the back door.

> CUT TO:

EXT. DITCH – NIGHT

Malkovich lands with a thud in the ditch. Craig is waiting there with his van. On its side is painted 'See The World in Malk-O-Vision' followed by a phone number. Malkovich is huddled and shivering and soaking wet. Mr Hiroshi falls into the ditch next to Malkovich.

CRAIG

So how was it?

MR HIROSHI

It was amazing this time!

MALKOVICH

That . . . was . . . no . . . simulation.

MR HIROSHI
(*noticing Malkovich*)
Oh my gosh, Mr Malkovich! It's such an honor to meet you!

CRAIG
(*to Malkovich*)
I know. I'm sorry . . .

Mr Hiroshi stands there, ignored and in awe, as Malkovich and Craig eye each other. Finally, he turns and heads to the open van. He takes a seat, fastens his seat belt, and waits patiently. Malkovich struggles to articulate his existential crisis.

MALKOVICH

I have been to the dark side. I have seen a world that no man should ever see.

CRAIG

Really? For most people it's a rather pleasant experience. What exactly did you . . .?

MALKOVICH

This portal is mine and it must be sealed up for ever. For the love of God.

CRAIG

With all respect, sir, I discovered that portal. It is my livelihood.

MALKOVICH

It's *my* head, Schwartz, and I'll see you in court!

Malkovich trudges off along the shoulder of the turnpike.

CRAIG
(*calling after him*)

And who's to say I won't be seeing what you're seeing . . . in court?

Cars whiz by Malkovich. Someone yells from a passing car.

MALKOVICH
(*voice-over*)

Hey, Malkovich! Think fast!

Malkovich looks up. A beer can comes flying out of the car and hits him on the head.

CUT TO:

INT. CRAIG AND LOTTE'S APARTMENT – NIGHT

Craig is feeding the animals. His gun is stuck in his pants. He gets to Lotte's cage. She is bound but ungagged. She looks haggard.

LOTTE
(*musing*)

Once this was a relationship based on love.

CRAIG

And you gave up your claim to that love the first time you stuck your dick in Maxine.

LOTTE

You fell in love with her first.

CRAIG

Yeah, but I didn't do anything about it. Out of respect for our marriage.

LOTTE

You didn't do anything about it out of respect for the fact that she wouldn't let you near her with a ten-foot pole, which is, by the way, about nine feet, nine inches off the mark anyway.

76

CRAIG
(*beat*)

That's true. Oh, God, Lotte, what have I become? My wife in a cage with a monkey. A gun in my hand. Betrayal in my heart.

LOTTE

Maybe this is what you've always been, Craig, you just never faced it before.

CRAIG

Perhaps you're right. I can't let you go through. Too much has happened. You're my ace in the hole.

LOTTE

I need a shower.

CRAIG
(*weepy*)

I'm sorry. Oh God, I'm sorry. I'm some kind of monster. I don't want to be a monster, Lot. I don't wanna.

LOTTE

You're not a monster, Craig. Just a confused man.

CRAIG

I love you so much.
(*dials phone, opens her cage, puts phone to her ear*)
But I gotta go now. I've got to go be Johnny.

MAXINE
(*phone voice*)

J.M. Inc. Be all that someone . . .

LOTTE

We have to meet.

MAXINE
(*phone voice*)

One hour.

Craig hangs up, tapes Lotte's mouth.

CRAIG

I'll tell you all about it when I get home.

Craig exits. Lotte fiddles with the ropes on her wrists. Elijah, slumped in the corner of the cage, blankly watches her moving hands. Suddenly his eyes narrow. Something is going on in his brain. We move slowly into his eyes.

DISSOLVE TO:

EXT. JUNGLE – DAY

It is a memory: blurry and overexposed, the color washed out. The sound of running feet, huffing, frantic breathing. We watch from up in a tree (Elijah's POV) as two men in safari suits chase a couple of chimps across the jungle floor. The chimps are screaming as the safari men tackle them and tie them up. The safari men laugh.

SAFARI MAN

Well, these monkeys ain't going nowheres. Let's get us a couple a brews 'fore the boss comes back . . .

The safari men leave the chimps on the ground. We descend from the trees to the ground next to the bound chimps. One of the chimps looks at the camera. He grunts and squeals.

CHIMP ONE

Subtitles: Son, untie your mother and me! Quickly! Before the great bald chimp-men return.

A small pair of chimp hands enter in to frame and struggle to untie the ropes, but to no avail. Chimp Two speaks.

CHIMP TWO

Subtitles: Hurry, Elijah!

SAFARI MAN

Why, you little bastard!

Elijah is wrestled to the ground amidst much screaming.

DISSOLVE TO:

INT. CRAIG AND LOTTE'S APARTMENT – NIGHT

Elijah shakes off the memory and looks determinedly at the ropes on Lotte's hands. He attempts to untie the knot. He works furiously and he succeeds. Lotte pulls the tape from her mouth.

LOTTE

Oh, Elijah, you are magnificent!

Elijah beams and screams for ecstatic joy. Lotte unlocks the cage, and dials the phone.

Maxine! Listen: It hasn't been me in John the last two times. Craig's had me locked up in the apartment. He made me call you at gunpoint. It's been him! Oh, God, it's been him!

MAXINE
(off-screen, beat, calmly)

Really? Well, you know, he's quite good. I'm surprised. Anyway, I have a session with Malkovich I have to attend. I'll speak with you soon.

LOTTE

But Maxine, I thought it was me you loved.

MAXINE
(off-screen)

I thought so too, doll. I guess we were mistaken. Bye-bye.

Maxine hangs up. Lotte is visibly shaken.

CUT TO:

EXT. NEW YORK CITY STREETS (MONTAGE) – NIGHT

It's raining. Lotte wanders the streets, hugging herself. A lost soul.

CUT TO:

INT. MALKOVICH'S APARTMENT – NIGHT

The doorbell rings. Malkovich answers it. Maxine stands there, dressed in an evening gown.

MALKOVICH

What the fuck do you want?

MAXINE

I can explain about the portal, darling.

MALKOVICH

Don't con me, Maxine. We're finished. I don't know who the hell you people are, but this insanity is now over.

MAXINE

Oh, shut up.
(*beat*)
Craig, darling, are you in there?

Malkovich tenses up, then he shakes his head in an awkward, puppet-like manner. When Malkovich speaks, it seems to be against his will.

MALKOVICH
(*labored*)
Yes. How'd you know it was me?

MAXINE

Lotte called me. She escaped your evil clutches.

MALKOVICH

I see. I'm sorry I did that, Maxine, but I really love you so much and I just didn't know how else to be with you.

Maxine considers this, then:

MAXINE

So apparently you can control this Malkovich fellow now.

MALKOVICH
(*proudly*)
I'm getting better all the time.

MAXINE

I'll say you are. Let's do it on his kitchen table, then make him eat an omelette off of it.

MALKOVICH
(*as Malkovich*)
No . . . damn . . . you.
(*as Craig*)
Oh shut up, you overrated sack of shit.

Malkovich (as Craig) looks at Maxine for approval. She smiles; he's doing well. Encouraged, he begins undressing, and does a lewd bump and grind while looking mortified. Maxine giggles. Malkovich (Craig) giggles wildly.

CUT TO:

INT. CAB – NIGHT

It's raining. We're looking through the windshield as the taxi approaches Lester's mansion.

EXT. LESTER'S MANSION – NIGHT

Lotte, soaking wet with straggly hair, steps out of the cab and walks up to Lester's front door. She knocks. After a moment, Lester answers. He doesn't recognize Lotte.

LESTER

Yes?

LOTTE

It's Lotte Schwartz, Dr Lester. Craig's wife.

LESTER

Oh, yes! Oh, my God, you'll catch your death out there. Look at you. You're soaking wet. Please, come in.

LOTTE

Thank you, sir.

CUT TO:

INT. LIVING-ROOM – A BIT LATER

Lotte, now in a white terrycloth robe, sits by the fireplace and sips tea.

LESTER

How's that?

LOTTE

Much better, thank you.

LESTER

Good. Now what brings you to my door on such an inhospitable night?

LOTTE
(*beat*)
Dr Lester, I have an unhealthy obsession with John Malkovich.

LESTER
The performer?

LOTTE
Yes.

LESTER
I see. And what prompted you to come to me with this issue?

LOTTE
Well, when I was here for dinner with my husband, I happened upon a room which seemed to be a sort of John Malkovich museum and I thought perhaps you would have some appreciation of my state of mind. I just needed to talk.

LESTER
You look so lovely and fragile, my dear, sitting there in my oversized man's robe.

LOTTE
Thank you, Dr Lester. Tell me, what is this strange power Malkovich exudes. You've got to help me understand. All I think about is wanting to be him.

LESTER
Wanting to what?

LOTTE
Wanting to be him. To be John Malkovich.

LESTER
I see.
(*studies her, looks her up and down, then nods slowly*)
Perhaps you can.

LOTTE
What do you mean?

You can be Malkovich, my dear, if you like. For the rest of his life.

Lotte looks confused. Lester leans on the mantel and stares into the fire.

LOTTE

But Dr Lester, how –

LESTER
(*waving her off*)

I am not Dr Lester, my dear. I am Captain Mertin. You see, there are seventeen of us who live in the being you know as Lester.
(*turns to face Lotte, then says hello in seventeen different intonations each time shaking Lotte's hand*)

Hello. Hello. Good evening. Hello. Greetings. *Bonjour*. Hello. Hi. Good Evening. Hello. Nice to meet you. Hello. Hello. Hello. Hello. Hello. Hiya.

LOTTE

I don't understand.

LESTER

It was ninety years ago that I discovered a strange portal . . .
(*second voice*)

Is it ninety years ago already?
(*first voice*)

Yes, it is.
(*second voice*)

Hmmm, time flies.
(*first voice*)

. . . and I discovered that the portal led to a 'vessel' body and that my friends and I would be able to live forever, by leaping from vessel to vessel.

LOTTE

Dr Lester is such a vessel?

LESTER

Oh, yes. Yes indeed. Here.
(*pulls big old book off shelf*)

I wrote this book.

(*flips through it*)
It's a vanity thing, self-published, but still it's kind of a fun little diversion . . .
(*finds a page*)
Okay, here we go. The life-cycle of the *Vesselis humanus* known as Lester.

Lester has opened the book to an old-fashioned chart illustrating the different stages in the development of the vessel. He points to an illustration of the Lester vessel as a child.

The vessel, until it reaches the age of sexual maturity is known as a *Larva*. To enter it at this stage would cause the entrant to be absorbed into the vessel's own psyche.

LOTTE
Absorbed? What does that mean?

LESTER
Held prisoner, if you will, in the host's brain. If my friends and I had entered the *Larval* Lester, we would've been lost forever inside him.

LOTTE
Oh, goodness.

LESTER
(*indicating picture of young adult Lester*)
Now, from adolescence until the age of forty-four, the vessel is called a *Pupa*. You say it.

LOTTE
Pupa.

LESTER
One can enter the *Pupa*, but cannot control it and will soon be ejected.

LOTTE
Spit out?

LESTER
In layman's terms, yes. Finally, on its forty-fourth birthday, the vessel is *Ripe*. It must be entered before midnight on that

day. After that, the portal closes to the *Ripe* vessel and leads to the new *Larval* vessel.

> LOTTE

So Malkovich is almost ripe?

> LESTER

And we will enter him then. Of course, along the way, in this life, we've made many new friends we'd like to bring with us . . .

Lester takes Lotte's hand and leads her into the room next door.

CUT TO

INT. SITTING-ROOM – CONTINUOUS

Lotte and Lester enter. A group of friendly-looking old people sit around sipping tea.

> LESTER
> (*to the old people*)

This is Lotte, everyone. She is a new friend of ours.

> OLD PERSON #1

Hello. I'm Bernice.

> LOTTE

Hi. Nice to meet you all.

> OLD PERSON #1

My granddaughter's your age. She lives in San Diego.

> LOTTE

Oh. I hear that's a wonderful town.

Lester and the old people look at each other. Small nods of the head pass between them.

> LESTER

We like you, Lotte. We can see you are a decent, kind woman. So we've decided to offer you a place in John Malkovich with us. If you like.

LOTTE

Forever?

LESTER

For the rest of his life. Then we'll all move on to the next vessel. It's a great adventure.

LOTTE
(beat)

Dr Lester . . . Dr *Lesters*, you're being so nice to me. So trusting. There's something I should tell you about the Malkovich vessel.

CUT TO:

INT. MALKOVICH'S BEDROOM – NIGHT

Malkovich and Maxine lie naked on the bed, looking quite relaxed. Malkovich is different now. He's more casual and enthusiastic, less austere. He's more like Craig.

MAXINE

You still there, sweets?

MALKOVICH

Yeah. I figured out how to hold on as long as I want. It was simply a matter of making friends with the Malkovich body. Rather than thinking of it as an enemy to be whipped into submission, I've begun imagining it to be a real expensive suit I enjoy wearing.

MAXINE
(little-girl pout)

Do a puppet show for me, Craig honey.

MALKOVICH

You mean with Malkovich?

MAXINE

I'd love to see your work.

MALKOVICH
(*pleased*)

Really? Yeah. Okay.

Malkovich leans over and kisses her, then gets up.

I'll do something I call 'Craig's Dance of Despair and Disillusionment'.

Malkovich performs the same dance that the Craig puppet did at the beginning of the film. It begins awkwardly, but becomes more assured and ultimately spectacular, complete with impossible somersaults and perspiring brow. He finishes by falling to his knees and weeping.

MAXINE
(*moved*)

That was incredible. You're brilliant!

MALKOVICH

You see, Maxine, it isn't just playing with dolls.

MAXINE

You're right, my darling, it's so much more. It's playing with people!

Malkovich kisses Maxine. She snuggles close to him.

MAXINE

Stay in him for ever?

MALKOVICH
(*as Malkovich, screaming*)

No!

(*as Craig, calmly*)
But how will we make a living, my love, if our clientele doesn't have access to our product?

MAXINE

Well, we'll have all the money in Malkovich's bank account, plus he still gets acting work occasionally.

MALKOVICH
(*as Malkovich, breaking through*)

No! Please!

> (as Craig, to Malkovich)

Shut up, will you? We're trying to think here.

> (to Maxine)

It is sort of like being a puppeteer. I like that about it.

MAXINE

No one would ever have to know it's not him.

MALKOVICH
> (an idea)

And I could use his existing notoriety to launch my own puppeteering career!

MAXINE

Oh, Craiggy, that's brilliant!

CUT TO:

INT. FILE ROOM – NIGHT

Maxine and Malkovich are filling the portal with cement. Suddenly Malkovich stops and runs to the office door screaming a bloodcurdling scream. He stops just as suddenly, begins to strangle himself.

MALKOVICH
> (Craig to Malkovich)

Shut up!

> (to Maxine)

Sorry, dear, I lost control for a minute.

MAXINE
> (kissing him)

It's okay, my sweet.

They go back to filling the portal. There is a sound of many shuffling feet in the hallway. The door flies open and the old people led by Lester and Lotte burst in. Malkovich and Maxine turn with a start.

LESTER

Aaaahhhh, the portal!

LOTTE
> (to Malkovich)

You bastard!

Lotte lunges for Malkovich. Lester grabs her arm, holds her back.

LESTER

No! Don't harm the vessel!

LOTTE

It's Craig in there, I can tell.

LESTER

I understand, but we must protect the vessel at all costs.
(*to Malkovich*)
Please, Craig, please step aside and allow us to have what is
rightfully ours.

MALKOVICH

Squatter's rights, Lester.

*Malkovich laughs. Maxine slips her arm through Malkovich's, joins
him in his laughter and glances triumphantly over at Lotte.*

MAXINE

Now excuse us, we have an entertainment legend to create.
To re-create.

Maxine kisses Malkovich on the cheek.

LESTER
(*to the cult members*)
Clear the way for them, my friends. They will be dealt with in
due time.

*The old people grumble and let Malkovich and Maxine exit. They then
converge on the sealed portal and begin clawing desperately at the quick-
drying cement. Fingers are scraped raw, and we see smears of blood and
skin on the rough gray surface.*

LOTTE

We could just all enter the portal and chase Craig out.

LESTER

He's too powerful, my dear. Look at the way he controls the
Pupa Malkovich. If we entered now, Schwartz would just jam
us all into Malkovich's unconscious mind. That could be ugly
and bad.

LOTTE
(*upset*)

So what do we do?

LESTER

We have until Malkovich's forty-fourth birthday to figure out a plan.

CUT TO:

INT. AGENT'S OFFICE – DAY

A slick-looking agent answers a buzzing phone.

AGENT

Of course, send him right in. Don't ever keep him waiting again. Do you understand?

Malkovich and Maxine enter. The agent stands, holds out his hand.

John! Great to see you! Sorry about the cunt at reception.

MALKOVICH

This is my fiancée, Maxine.

The agent shakes Maxine's hand.

AGENT

Great to see you, Maxine. Sorry about the cunt at reception. Please have a seat.

Malkovich and Maxine sit.

Can I get you anything? Coffee? Water?

MAXINE

No thanks.

AGENT
(*into phone*)

Teresa, get me a chicken soup.
(*to Malkovich and Maxine*)

Chicken soup?

Maxine and Malkovich shake their heads 'no'.

MALKOVICH

I'll get right to the point, Larry. I'm a puppeteer now . . .

AGENT

Okay. Great.

MALKOVICH

. . . and I want to redirect my career so that from now on the name John Malkovich will be synonymous with puppets.

AGENT

Sure, sure. No problemo. Poof, you're a puppeteer. Heh heh. Just let me make a couple of calls.

CUT TO:

INT. BLACK BACKGROUND SET

C.U. of Malkovich being interviewed.

MALKOVICH

There's the truth and there are lies. Art always tell the truth.
(*puckish grin*)
Even when it's lying.

CUT TO:

TITLE: AMERICAN MASTERS PRESENTS

JOHN HORATIO MALKOVICH: DANCE OF DESPAIR AND DISILLUSIONMENT

DISSOLVE TO:

SEQUENCE OF BLACK-AND-WHITE STILL PHOTOGRAPHS:

EVANSTON, ILLINOIS IN THE 1950S, A WOMAN HOLDING A BABY, A YOUNG BOY ON A PONY

NARRATOR
(*voice-over*)
John Malkovich was born in Evanston, Illinois on December 16, 1954.

INT. JOHNSON HEYWARD'S OFFICE – DAY

C.U. of Johnson Heyward, 50, distinguished, being interviewed.

CHYRON: JOHNSON HEYWARD, MALKOVICH BIOGRAPHER

HEYWARD

His father abandoned the family early on and John was raised by his mother. He was a quiet boy, forever lost in the world of make-believe. He loved dolls, which at the time was viewed by his peers as effeminate. But now we can look back and see it was simply his life's work germinating.

CUT TO:

SEQUENCE OF STILL PHOTOGRAPHS OF YOUNG ADULT MALKOVICH IN VARIOUS PROFESSIONS

NARRATOR
(voice-over)

But it took Malkovich some years to discover what his life's work was. After graduating from Northwestern University with a degree in ethnomusicology, Malkovich floundered through a series of dead-end careers: salesman, laborer, film actor, typist, finally finding his calling in puppetry . . .

INT. CATSKILL RESORT – DAY

Home-video shot of Malkovich performing puppetry at a Catskill resort. Malkovich dangles the Craig puppet in front of him. He is nervous in front of the borscht-belt audience.

MALKOVICH
(uncertainly)

Um . . . *shalom aleichem,* ladies and gentlemen, my name is . . . John Malkovich. It's the emmis . . . I'm really John Malkovich.
(out-of-control giggle, then:)
You probably have seen me in many motion pictures, which were fun for me to act in . . . But now I enjoy doing

puppetry. And so that's what I'm going to perform for you wonderful people today.

Malkovich turns on a tape recorder. Eerie zither music fills the hall. He begins to work the puppet. It bows solemnly to the audience.

In this world there are . . . *Twenty-One Ways to Die*. Some are easy and some are hard, but all . . . are fatal. Arsenic poisoning.

The Craig puppet starts to stagger around, clutching its throat. Gagging sounds play over the zither music. The puppet collapses in the throes of death.

Drowning.

As if in water, the Craig puppet flails, hands waving over its head. Splashing and gasping sounds play over the zither music. The puppet stops struggling, then floats in a dead man's pose.

Falling from a tall building.

The puppet takes a swan dive and falls head first (staying suspended in one place), its arms flailing. The whistling sound of something plummeting is heard over the music. Finally the whistling ends in a meaty, bone-shattering crash as the puppet lands in a heap on the floor.

The audience is unresponsive.

NARRATOR
(*voice-over*)

But from these inauspicious beginnings captured on home video, Malkovich's ascent as a puppeteer was fast and furious. Within months of this performance he was being touted as arguably the greatest puppeteer in the history of the world.

CUT TO:

INT. MANTINI'S OFFICE – DAY

C.U. of Derek Mantini, looking a bit like magician David Copperfield.

CHYRON: DEREK MANTINI, PUPPETEER

MANTINI
Malkovich is a fabulous technician. And he's certainly a

worthy competitor for the title of greatest puppeteer in the history of the world. I'm sure we'll work together some day soon. And I look forward to that collaboration.

CUT TO:

INT. THEATRE STAGE – NIGHT

Video clip of Malkovich on-stage working his Craig Schwartz puppet before rapt black-tie audience.

> NARRATOR
> (*voice-over*)
> Malkovich's rise to fame brought about a renaissance in the art of puppeteering. He began teaching the now overflowing puppetry master class at New York's notorious Juilliard School.

CUT TO:

INT. WORKSHOP STAGE – DAY

Malkovich in black T-shirt, directing a group of puppeteering students in a workshop. One student stands on-stage working a marionette. Malkovich distractedly chews his fingernails as he watches. Finally he hops up on to the stage and angrily pulls the puppet from the young man's hands.

> MALKOVICH
> No. No. What are you doing? What? What?

> STUDENT
> I'm making him weep, John.

> MALKOVICH
> Well, that's your problem, isn't it? You're *making* him weep, but you *yourself* are not *weeping*. Don't ever fuck with your audience. Until the puppet is an extension of you, it's just a novelty act. It's Topo Gigio. Nothing more.
> (*emphatically to other students*)
> Do you see what I'm saying?

The seated students nod appreciatively.

Here, watch this . . .

94

Malkovich takes the student's puppet and makes it weep. It's magnificent.

                                                    CUT TO:

INT. LOFT – NIGHT

An amazing place with twenty-foot ceilings and a panoramic view of New York. Malkovich (Craig) lounges in silk pajamas, sipping champagne and watching the TV biography. He is enjoying it immensely. Next to him on an end table are framed wedding photos of Maxine and him.

                        MALKOVICH
                         (*calling*)
            Honey, it's on! You're missing it!

                                                    CUT TO:

INT. NURSERY – NIGHT

Maxine is hanging some cute pictures of ducks on the wall. She is quite pregnant.

                          MAXINE
                        (*muttering*)
            I'm busy.

                        MALKOVICH
                        (*voice-over*)
            It's really good! I look really fucking amazing. I'd fuck me!
                 (*trying to engage her, make her laugh*)
            Hey, maybe there's a way to do that. Huh?

Maxine wipes her sweaty brow and stares out the window.

                                                    CUT TO:

NEWS FOOTAGE OF MALKOVICH SHAKING HANDS WITH THE
PRESIDENT

                          NARRATOR
                        (*voice-over*)
            Malkovich was the toast of the town . . . from the beltway . . .
            to Broadway!

STILL PHOTOGRAPH OF MALKOVICH'S CRAIG PUPPET TAP-
DANCING ALONGSIDE SAVION GLOVER

CUT TO:

EXT. SUBURBAN STREET – NIGHT

*A group of children trick or treating. Three in the group are wearing full
over-the-head John Malkovich masks.*

> NARRATOR
> (*voice-over*)
> The John Malkovich mask was the most popular costume of
> this Hallowe'en season. His now famous *alter ego*, the Craig
> Schwartz puppet, coming in a close second.

CUT TO:

EXT. SUBURBAN STREET – NIGHT

*Shot of kid dressed as Craig Schwartz, dancing like a puppet and
waving at the camera.*

CUT TO:

SHOT OF MALKOVICH AND MAXINE ATTENDING SOME PREMIÈRE.

> NARRATOR
> (*voice-over*)
> But John Malkovich didn't make this transition from
> journeyman actor to star puppeteer alone. By his side
> throughout the entire process was his wife and manager,
> Maxine Lund.

CUT TO:

INT. JOHNSON HEYWARD'S OFFICE – DAY

C.U. of Johnson Heyward, being interviewed.

> HEYWARD
> Oh, Maxine is definitely the driving force behind Malkovich.

INT. LESTER'S MANSION – NIGHT

Lester, Lotte in pajamas, Elijah and several old people watch the documentary. We see Lotte's caged animals in the background.

HEYWARD

She's a human dynamo. She loved her husband so much, she was able to say, 'Hey, take this chance. Do what you love. I will support you.'

Lotte screams and throws a pillow at the TV set.

LESTER
(*kissing her on the forehead*)
Relax, my dear. This travesty will all be over by morning.

CUT TO:

INT. LOFT – NIGHT

Malkovich watches the documentary. It's coming to a close.

NARRATOR
(*voice-over*)
And what does the future hold for John Horatio Malkovich? Well, to quote the bard, he's got the world on a string.

MUSIC: *'World on a String' sung by Frank Sinatra*

Malkovich clicks off the TV.

MALKOVICH

Max, it's over! I gotta head down to ABT. Doing that *Swan Lake* benefit tonight! Remember? We'll celebrate Malkovich's big four-four when I get home! Okay?
(*trying a joke*)
Jesus, why couldn't I find a portal to a younger body? Hope I don't fall and break my hip tonight! Ha, ha!

There is no response. Malkovich sighs, gets up, goes into the nursery.

CUT TO:

INT. NURSERY – CONTINUOUS

Malkovich enters, watches Maxine, who doesn't look up as she is spreading a colorful little blanket in the bassinet.

> MALKOVICH
> *(after a moment, gently trying to connect)*
> Should I bring some sweets? A birthday cake? Funny hats?
> We can make him do the limbo to celebrate.

> MAXINE
> *(not looking up)*
> No, that's okay. I'm probably going to turn in early.

> MALKOVICH
> Okay.

CUT TO:

EXT. LINCOLN CENTER – NIGHT

Malkovich enters the Met Opera stage door.

CUT TO:

INT. LOFT – NIGHT

Maxine sits on the living-room floor and plays some soft lullaby music on to her pregnant belly with a Sony My First Tape Recorder.

INT. MET OPERA AUDITORIUM – NIGHT

The house is packed with a black-tie crowd. A life-size version of the Craig puppet performs Swan Lake *with the corps of the American Ballet Theater. It is quite lovely. A ballerina leaps into the puppet's arms. Amazingly it catches her. The audience erupts with cries of 'bravo'.*

CUT TO:

INT. APARTMENT HALLWAY – LATER

Malkovich whistles as he walks down the hall carrying his Craig puppet in what looks like a bass violin case, except that it is shaped like a man.

He hears the phone ringing in his apartment. He fiddles with the lock and opens his front door.

CUT TO:

INT. LOFT – CONTINUOUS

Malkovich studies the room, trying to understand. Glass and debris all over the floor.

The wind howls. The little tape recorder sits amid the debris still playing a lullaby. The phone rings. Malkovich grabs it.

> MALKOVICH
> (*urgently*)

Yes? Hello?

> VOICE

We have Maxine.

> MALKOVICH

Oh my God. Listen, don't hurt her. However much you want . . .

> VOICE

No, you listen, asshole. I don't want money. What I want is for you to leave John Malkovich. *Now.*

> MALKOVICH
> (*beat*)

Who is this? Lester?

> VOICE

Does it matter? We are going to kill Maxine if you do not leave the body immediately.

Malkovich paces.

> MALKOVICH
> (*thinking aloud*)

I can't do that. If I leave Malkovich, I'm Craig Schwartz again. I have no career, no money. Maxine would no longer have anything to do with me. I mean, as it is, she barely has anything to do with me now. So what's my incentive to make this sacrifice?

VOICE

Jesus, we're going to kill your wife, you fucking lunatic!

MALKOVICH
(*the pressure*)

Oh God.

(*beat*)

I can't leave.

Malkovich hangs up. He stares at the phone. He blasts the stereo, begins cleaning up the debris. He picks up the little tape recorder and turns it off.

CUT TO:

INT. LESTERCORP MAILROOM – CONTINUOUS

Lester listens to a dial tone. Old people and Lotte huddle around, all of them dressed up in their fanciest traveling clothes.

LESTER

He called our bluff.

LOTTE

Shit. *Shit!*

Lotte glances through the cracked door at Maxine sitting on the floor in the file room.

These people are just ruining everything! They just ruin everything all the time!

Lester strokes Lotte's hair, kisses her on the forehead. He looks at the clock on the wall. It's 10.40.

LESTER

We have until midnight to figure something out, darling.

Lotte looks into Lester's eyes, kisses him on the lips and pulls away. She seems to be entering some sort of altered state of resolve. Intensely focused, she enters the file room.

INT. FILE ROOM – CONTINUOUS

Lotte faces Maxine. The two just watch each other, Lotte in a steely trance. Slowly she pulls Craig's gun from her pocket. Maxine gasps, scans the room for a way out. There is none. Except the portal. She leaps into it. Lotte snaps back into reality.

> LOTTE

Fuck!

CUT TO:

INT. LESTERCORP MAILROOM/FILE ROOM – CONTINUOUS

Lester hears Lotte's exclamation and glances into the file room in time to see Lotte diving into the portal, gun in hand.

> LESTER

Lotte, no! We can't *really* kill her! She's carrying –

The portal door slams shut.

– Malkovich's seed! Our next vessel!

But Lotte's gone. Lester and the old people exchange distraught looks.

CUT TO:

INT. PORTAL – CONTINUOUS

Maxine heaves as she crawls through the slime. Lotte is behind her.

> LOTTE

You're not getting away, Maxine.

> MAXINE

Lotte, please, you don't under . . .

A sucking sound. The two get pulled forward. A flash of light.

CUT TO:

INT. BEDROOM – MORNING

It's a 1950s room and has the washed-out quality of an old color photograph. In bed, having sweaty, violent sex, are John Malkovich's thirty-year-old parents. We see that Malkovich's father is a young version of Lester. John Malkovich as a little boy stands in the doorway watching unobserved. He clutches a baby doll to his chest and looks scared and confused. Suddenly Lotte and Maxine pop into the room.

Unlike their surroundings, they appear in full, saturated color. They both look around. Malkovich and his parents are unaware of them.

> MAXINE

Where the hell am I?

> LOTTE

Malkovich's unconscious – the last thing you'll ever see, bitch.

Lotte lifts the pistol and trains it on Maxine. Suddenly, Mrs Malkovich notices John in the doorway. She gasps, pushes her husband off of her, pulls the sheet to her chest.

Mr Malkovich turns over to see what's going on. Lotte is distracted by the scene.

> MALKOVICH AS A LITTLE BOY

Daddy, why are you hurting Mommy?

> MRS MALKOVICH

Daddy's not hurting me, Johnny. We were just playing.

> MALKOVICH AS A LITTLE BOY

Can I play, too?

Mr and Mrs Malkovich hesitate, not knowing how to respond. Maxine dives out the window. Lotte snaps back into focus and dives after her.

CUT TO:

INT. SCHOOL LOCKER ROOM – DAY

Maxine runs past a naked, humiliated, junior-high-school-age Malkovich being led by a burly gym teacher past jeering, bigger, more developed boys. Lotte appears in the midst of this and gives chase.

CUT TO:

INT. BASEMENT – DAY

Maxine lands in this dark, dank room, crowded with boxes and discarded furniture. She runs past as little John Malkovich is facing the wall, sitting in a child-sized rocking chair, rocking with jerky, rhythmic intensity, and whimpering penitently.

MALKOVICH AS A LITTLE BOY
I am bad I am bad I am bad I am bad I am bad I am bad . . .

Lotte appears, runs past the tragic young Malkovich.

CUT TO:

INT. WOMAN'S BATHROOM – NIGHT

Malkovich enters, closes the door, locks it, checks the cabinet under the sink, finds a hamper and starts rifling through it. Maxine plops into the closed room just as Malkovich pulls out a pair of panties and holds them enthusiastically to his nose. Maxine looks for an escape route. Lotte appears. Maxine exits. Lotte follows.

CUT TO:

INT. APARTMENT – NIGHT

A younger adult Malkovich is sitting on the couch with a pretty, smart-looking young woman. He's in a beret and trying to impress her.

MALKOVICH
I've always felt that in *The Stranger, Camus* [*pronounced Cay-mus*] was trying to elicit –

SMART WOMAN
Who?

MALKOVICH
(*flushing*)
Albert Cay-mus?

Maxine runs through the room followed by a gun-wielding Lotte.

SMART WOMAN
It's Camus.

MALKOVICH
(*mortified*)
Oh.

INT. SCHOOL BUS – DAY

Young John Malkovich sits crying by himself in the back of the bus as the other kids taunt him.

> KIDS
> (*chanting*)
> Little Johnny Malk-o-pee / wet his pants so all could see . . .

Maxine appears in the aisle, gets her bearings, starts to run. Lotte appears behind her, leaps and tackles Maxine. The two wrestle on the floor for possession of the gun.

> . . . no one smells as much as he / Little Johnny Malkopee . . .

Maxine and Lotte have rolled down the front steps of the bus. Maxine is halfway out the door. Her head is dangerously close to the street speeding by below. Both tumble out the door.

> CUT TO:

EXT. DITCH – NIGHT

Maxine and Lotte fall together into the ditch. It's pouring rain. The gun flies from Lotte's hand as she hits the ground. Maxine scrambles for it, gets it, stands and points it at Lotte. The two watch each other, wild-eyed and panting. After a bit, Lotte speaks.

> LOTTE
> I loved you so much. Why did you have to hurt me like that?

Maxine looks long and hard at Lotte.

> MAXINE
> I'm sorry, Lotte. I was wrong. I'm truly sorry.

> LOTTE
> I loved you! I loved you!

> MAXINE
> (*beat*)
> I guess I loved you too. In my way.

> LOTTE
> You are so full of shit, Maxine.

MAXINE
(*apologetically*)

I know.
>   (*beat, looks up at the sky, then back down at Lotte*)

It's your baby, okay? Okay?!

LOTTE

What?

MAXINE

The baby. It's yours. It's ours. I got pregnant when you were
in Malkovich.

LOTTE

You can't fuck with me any more, Maxine.

MAXINE

It's true, damn it! Look . . . remember the time the condom
broke?

Lotte does. She remains silent.

I kept the baby because I knew you were the father . . . the
other mother . . . whatever. Because it was yours.

LOTTE
(*beat, slight smile*)

So, we're parents? Together?
>   (*then, angry*)

You never would've told me unless this happened.

MAXINE

I didn't know how. I knew you hated me. I wanted to. I think
about you all the time. I wanted to.

They look at each other.

CUT TO:

INT. BAR – NIGHT

*It's a dive. Malkovich (Craig) sits there drinking heavily. He's a weepy
mess. Another drunk guy staggers up to him.*

DRUNK

Say, aren't you John Malpisich?

MALKOVICH
(*beat*)

No.

DRUNK

You are! You are! You can't fool me!
(*to others, pointing*)
John Malpisich! John Malpisich!

MALKOVICH

No, I'm not. I am not John Malpisich. Fuck you, fuck you!
Fuck you all!

Malkovich lunges at the drunk, and the two wrestle on the floor. A crowd of drunks gathers around them and starts chanting.

DRUNKS

Malkovich! Malkovich! Malkovich! Malkovich! . . .

The bartender pulls Malkovich off the drunk. As he's getting pulled away, Malkovich kicks the drunk one last time in the head. The circle of drunks widens.

MALKOVICH

I am not Malkovich.

He walks off determinedly toward the back of the bar.

CUT TO:

INT. LESTERCORP MAILROOM – CONTINUOUS

Lester holds a phone to his ear.

LESTER

Yes?

MALKOVICH
(*phone voice*)
Don't do it! For the love of God, please don't kill Maxine!

LESTER

So you'll leave?

MALKOVICH
(*phone voice*)

Yes. I'll leave.

LESTER

All right then. Do it now over the phone so I can hear, and
your lovely bride walks.

CUT TO:

INT. BAR – CONTINUOUS

Malkovich is on a payphone.

MALKOVICH

Okay. I'm going.

*Malkovich's face strains. He slumps over, then regains consciousness.
He is Malkovich again.*

I'm free! I'm free!

CUT TO:

INT. LESTERCORP MAILROOM/FILE ROOM – CONTINUOUS

Lester, holding the phone, yells to the other old people.

LESTER

Now, my friends! The time is now!

*The old people hurry into the file room. An old lady straightens her
husband's tie. Lester pauses for a moment.*

Lotte.

*Lester checks the clock: 11.55. He can't wait, and he follows the other
old people.*

CUT TO:

INT. BAR – NIGHT

Malkovich, on the verge of tears, studies himself in a mirrored beer sign.

> MALKOVICH
> I'm free! I'm back! I'm Malko . . .

Malkovich's body jerks crazily around, like he's being riddled with bullets, as the old people enter him. The drunks at the bar watch.

> (*sounding like Lester*)
> . . . We're Malkovich. At last.

CUT TO:

EXT. NEW JERSEY TURNPIKE DITCH – NIGHT

A soaking-wet, anxious Craig lies in the ditch, disoriented. Next to him is the piece of molding. He raises his head, peers around and sees Lotte and Maxine hitching together by the side of the road. A look of confusion passes over his face: What are they doing here? What are they doing here together? It's probably not good, but he's going to make the best of it. He hurries over to them.

> CRAIG
> Max! Lotte!

He tries to embrace Maxine. She pushes him away. He looks hurt. He turns to Lotte.

> Lotte, long time! You look great!

He tries to kiss Lotte on the cheek. She moves her head. He turns back to Maxine.

> Maxine, I just left Malkovich for you. It's not worth being in Malkovich without you, so I . . .

A car has stopped. Lotte opens the door. She and Maxine get in.

> MAXINE
> (*to driver*)
> He's not with us.

The door closes and the car pulls away. Craig runs after it.

CRAIG
(*screaming*)

I did the right thing! It proves I love you! It proves it! Doesn't
it? I gave it all up for you, Maxine! Maxine! Maxine! Don't
you see, I gave up everything. Please! I'm wet and I'm cold!
And I'm Craig! I'm nothing again!
(*beat, screaming*)

Damn it!

CUT TO:

INT. CAR – NIGHT

*Maxine and Lotte sit together in the back seat. A couple of Jersey guys
heading into the city for a night of drinking are in the front. The music
is loud. Maxine takes Lotte's hand. Lotte smiles, Maxine puts Lotte's
hand on her pregnant belly.*

LOTTE

What should we name her?

MAXINE

How dreary – to be – Somebody / How public – like a frog /
To tell one's name – the livelong June / To an admiring Bog!

LOTTE

That's Emily Dickinson, isn't it?

MAXINE
(*pleased*)

Yeah. It is.

(*kisses Lotte*)

Let's call her Emily.

LOTTE

Let's!

*The guys in the front are bobbing to the music. Maxine and Lotte giggle
about this. Lotte sighs contentedly and looks out the window.*

CUT TO:

EXT. BAR – NIGHT

The streets are empty and wet with rain. Malkovich exits the bar and walks toward the camera, which is at a low angle. He is cool now, regal. When he fills the frame, he stops, looks off for a moment feeling the majesty and power of this young, healthy body. Then he is gone.

CUT TO:

INT. BUS – NIGHT

Craig is wet and dirty and crazed. He is rambling on to the person sitting next to him, who is pretending to read a book.

CRAIG
. . . so I clearly did the right thing but that didn't fucking matter to her . . . but she'll see, cause I'm heading right back into Malkovich now, *right now*, and I'll fucking throw Lester out. There's no way he's a match for me, cause keep in mind I was the only one strong enough to control Malkovich . . . when nobody else could, right? So Maxine is gonna be real sorry real fast, cause suddenly I'm rich and famous again and she's poor and living in some dump with chimps and . . . birds and other shit . . . Y'know?

CUT TO:

EXT. NYC STREET – NIGHT

Craig runs toward the Mertin-Flemmer building.

CUT TO:

INT. 7½ FLOOR – NIGHT

Craig stands outside LesterCorp, trying to get in. He no longer has a key. He grabs a fire extinguisher from the wall and throws it at the glass office front. It shatters. Craig runs through.

CUT TO:

INT. FILE ROOM – NIGHT

Craig pulls open the portal door and dives in. The clock reads 12.35.

CUT TO:

INT. PORTAL – CONTINUOUS

Craig scurries through. The walls of the portal look different now, still membranous but a lighter color, somehow the membrane now looks youthful and fresh. Craig doesn't seem to notice. He gets sucked through.

FADE OUT:

FADE IN:

EXT./INT. LESTER'S MANSION – DAY

Charlie Sheen, visibly older, almost bald now, with a fringe of hair around the sides of his head, knocks on the door. After a moment, the door opens and we see Malkovich, also visibly older, but with a toupee of lush hair.

MALKOVICH

Machine!

CHARLIE SHEEN

Malcatraz!

The two embrace. Charlie Sheen enters, Malkovich entwines his arm through Charlie Sheen's and the two walk down the hall.

MALKOVICH

So how's Celeste?

CHARLIE SHEEN

Good, good. She's sorry she couldn't make it today, but she had to go to the store.

MALKOVICH

That's fine. I wanted to talk to you both, but we'll just talk. Okay?

CHARLIE SHEEN

Cool. Great.

Charlie Sheen and Malkovich approach Floris from behind. She is in a kimono and watering plants. Malkovich kisses her on the back of the neck as he passes. She giggles, shoos him away playfully, turns and sees Charlie Sheen.

FLORIS
Charlie! I didn't even hear the door!

She pecks him on the cheek.

CHARLIE SHEEN
Lookin' great, Flor.

FLORIS
I'm looking grateful?

Charlie Sheen and Malkovich laugh appreciatively. Floris looks confused.

They enter the kitchen.

CUT TO:

INT. LESTER'S KITCHEN – CONTINUOUS

It's bright and cheerful. Malkovich pours two cups of carrot juice, hands one to Charlie Sheen.

MALKOVICH
(*beat*)
Charlie, I feel like you and I and Floris and Celeste have become so close over the last several years.

CHARLIE SHEEN
We feel the same way, buddy. Amigos.

MALKOVICH
And we don't want to lose you guys.

CHARLIE SHEEN
What are you talking about? You're not going to lose us.

MALKOVICH
Eventually we will.

CUT TO:

INT. LESTER'S HALLWAY – CONTINUOUS

Malkovich and Charlie Sheen walk up the stairs.

MALKOVICH
Look at us, we're not getting any younger.

CHARLIE SHEEN
Don't rub it in.

Malkovich leads Charlie Sheen out of the kitchen.

MALKOVICH
Listen, Char, this is gonna sound crazy, but I found this way
for us to live for ever. All of us.

CHARLIE SHEEN
What are you talking about, Johnny-boy?

MALKOVICH
All of us. You, me, Floris, Celeste, Gary Sinise, maybe.

CHARLIE SHEEN
I don't understand.

*They've arrived at a closed door. Malkovich opens it, ushers Charlie
Sheen in.*

CUT TO:

INT. LESTER'S ROOM – CONTINUOUS

*Malkovich and Charlie Sheen are in the room. Malkovich switches on
the light.*

MALKOVICH
Charlie, this is Emily.

*The photos of Malkovich have been taken down and replaced with
photos of a seven-year-old girl. We see surveillance photos of her at
different ages, with and without Maxine and Lotte. We see report cards,
blown-up little-girl diary entries, family trees, etc. It's very similar to the
way it looked when it was filled with Malkovich stuff, but now there's
lots of empty wall space, because this vessel is still so young. Charlie
Sheen looks at Malkovich, confused and freaked out.*

EXT. COMMUNITY SWIMMING-POOL – DAY

It's a beautiful, sunny day. Maxine, Lotte and Emily sit on towels, poolside, the remains of a picnic lunch scattered about. Emily plays with an Etch-a-Sketch.

> LOTTE
> (*to Maxine*)
> Y'know, it's weird, I had a dream about Craig last night.

We see Emily's eye twitch involuntarily at the word 'Craig'.

> MAXINE
> You're kidding. Blast from the past.

> EMILY
> Who's Craig, mom?

Lotte and Maxine exchange looks.

> MAXINE
> Who's Craig?

Emily's eye twitches again at the name. We now shift into a POV, looking out through Emily's eyes. It's not the girl's POV, but the POV of someone deep inside her head. Most of the screen is dark and the little we do see looks far away and dim. The voices are muffled.

> Well . . .

> LOTTE
> Um, he's a man your mom and I were married to, Em!

> EMILY
> (*off-screen*)
> Really? You guys were married to a man? Yech.

> MAXINE
> Before you were born, honey. Before your mom and I knew each other.

We switch out of POV.

EMILY

Oh. So can I swim yet?

MAXINE
(*checking watch*)
Yes ma'am, I guess it's been long enough.

EMILY

Yay!

Emily runs off.

LOTTE

That went surprisingly well.

Lotte and Maxine smile at each other, relieved. They kiss. Emily is now at the edge of the pool shouting gleefully at her parents.

EMILY

Mom! Mom! Mom! Mom! Look at me! Watch! Watch! Watch this!

Maxine and Lotte turn their attention to Emily. She yells and jumps, cannonball-style into the pool, making a big splash. We follow her underwater as she swims through water-filtered sunlight and the legs of other playing children. We shift to the POV deep inside Emily's head.

FADE OUT